ACCIDENTAL COWGIRL RIDES AGAIN

More Stories of a City Slicker's Life on an Eastern Oregon Ranch

Kristy St. Clair

ACCIDENTAL COWGIRL RIDES AGAIN

Photographs
Front cover;
Kristy St. Clair, 2013
(by Phil St. Clair)
***

Interior page:
Kristy and Phil St. Clair
at the cabin in Poison Creek, 2013
(by Jim Shields)

Cover
Created by Mark Highberger
Wallowa, Oregon

ISBN:
13: 978-1495290619
10:1495290611

With love, this book is dedicated to Phil. Friend, lover, husband, in that order. To my mom and dad, and to Phil's parents, all of whom made ranch life possible.

And to the ones who have gone before me: family, friends, dogs, cats, and horses. Save a place for me at the ranch above. Hopefully, that's where I'll end up.

Acknowledgments

Thank you to my inspiring editor, Sandy Raschke. She patiently guided me via email with her vast expertise and made me enthusiastic again when I was flagging. I am grateful to Kelly Cooper for introducing me to her. And thanks to my first editor, Mark Highberger, who had no idea what he was getting into when he took me on. A patient teacher, he never settled for mediocre writing. Last, I am forever grateful to my three proof readers, Dixie Lund, Les Zaitz, and Lee Juillerat.

Specifically, thank you to the Izee ranchers, past and present: the Keerins, Officers, Hydes, Rickmans, Schnabeles, Holidays, Bedorthas, Martins, Swindlehursts, Wegners, Dianne, Bidwells, Nelsons, Andersons, Hodges, and Browns. I pray this book, like the first one, reveals the awe and respect I have for your intelligence, work ethic, and generosity of spirit. Please accept my gratitude for allowing us to hang around all of you and soak up your knowledge.

Also, to all our much loved friends on the fringes: the Cernazanus, Moores, Southworths, Dave Traylor, Hugh Farrell, Cernys, Olivers, Mark Bovingdon, Aasnesses, Jake and Amanda, Barkers, DeRoys, DesJardins, Cronins, Kate, Stinnetts, Zinns, Robertsons, all the folks, now and in the past, at the Grant County Soil and Water Conservation Service, Delanos, Leslie Walker, Gilmores, Tom Winter, Tom Hunt, Paladijczuks, Wilkinsons, Thompsons, Hueckmans, Galbreaths, Traftons, Neals, and Unterwegners. And to "the boys." If I left anyone out, please chalk it up to early dementia. All of these people encouraged me. A special thanks to Billy Bird, wherever you are.

To our families. For all your help and support during the years. The ranch supplied the background for loads of memories. Love to all of you.

Finally, to the four funsters: Phil, Wade, Gabe and Jim, who were here, off and on, making the journey worthwhile. ◆◆

Kristy and Phil St. Clair at the cabin on Poison Creek in Izee

CONTENTS

CONTENTS (Continued)

PREFACE

In my first memoir, *Accidental Cowgirl, A City Slicker's Life on an Eastern Oregon Ranch*, the stories I told were all about first experiences—first cattle drive, first rattlesnake encounter, first tree (and *only* tree so far) that fell on Phil—those singular events. Hopefully, the reader realized the title "accidental cowgirl" is the exact opposite of what I was and what I am—at least the "cowgirl" part. I'm a complete 'fraidy cat, and chicken when it comes to horses. They are lovely animals, but I never felt safe on a horse's back. And, in the thirty-nine years of living in Izee, that hasn't changed.

As in the first book, the following chapters are meant to make fun of myself and to show how each experience (except the horse thing) changed me. *Us.* How we quickly learned to become independent in some areas, such as figuring the best way to move a herd overland on—*yes*—horseback, fixing a vehicle, getting frozen plumbing to work in the dead of winter, or cutting down a juniper without getting squashed. However, on occasion, we had to ask for help from our neighbors; for example, doctoring cows—because we couldn't just guess or tinker with one as if it were a pickup. Our lack of knowledge and understanding, as to what cows needed or how their internal structure works, could have led to disaster and loss. Sure, some of the cow tending we learned on the fly or through pure intuition. But other bovine matters? Well, that's where the ranchers, our neighbors, entered the picture and these stories took root.

Accidental Cowgirl Rides Again was written to expand upon our experiences and relationships with them, our friends, and family visitors. Yet, there are still stories left untold and many people we've met along the way, unmentioned. That's not to say that they aren't important, or that there won't be a third incarnation of *Accidental Cowgirl* sometime in the future. It's just that these chapters are highlights from the past that leapt out at me like a 3-D movie. They begged to be written. So I did. ♦♦

THE END AND THE BEGINNING

From city slicker to accidental cowgirl ...

The End and the Beginning

"Mike, are you saying Dad could have paid the weed-spraying bill and avoided the sheriff's sale?" I asked. "This is about obliterating a weed?"

"Yep, the lien happened because Paul underestimated the magnitude and seriousness of his Whitetop weed problem. It takes over hay land and spreads to neighbors' properties," said Mike Jennings, my father's rumpled attorney. "The county sprayed it for him then sent him a bill. Your dad ignored the county's bill. His contract with the previous owner, Don Jones, stipulates that if a tax lien is attached to the property Mr. Jones can foreclose and demand the balance. So the ranch will be sold day after tomorrow at the auction."

"Do we need to move off the ranch?" asked Phil, getting down to business while fetching a cup of coffee for Mike. "Who'll look after Paul's cattle and horses?"

"*You* will for now," Mike said, his voice echoing from the pillowy depths of a 1930's sofa of Dad's. "The estate has six months to redeem the property even if someone else buys it at the sale. Since you're the executrix of Paul's estate, Kristy, you both can stay on the ranch during that time.

"Executrix?" I said. "He never told me."

"Not surprising. He was cagey about his personal business," Mike said, climbing out of the cushions to reach his brown leather briefcase for papers. "In fact, the estate's a mess. I tried to get him prepared for the future." Mike handed each of us a copy of the estate documents.

"I know. He thought he was immortal," I said. "No doubt Dad believed he had two or three decades left."

"Well, I don't mean any disrespect," said Mike, "but Paul's dying was lousy timing. See on that line where he owed $600,000.00 to creditors? But on this line his assets are $200,000.00," he said. "He hadn't filed state or federal income tax in ten years. The story is that the I.R.S. waited, thinking he'd hit it big someday.

"So from the assets, the I.R.S., the hospital, his lawyer, and the executrix get paid first. Then the creditors get a percentage of what's left over. All that aside, do you think you could get up the money to redeem?"

2

"Oh sure," said Phil. "Two ex-hippies with twenty dollars in our checking account and zero savings. Unless someone buys the ranch and pays us to work on it, we'll be gone in six months."

"Well," said Mike. "Let's see what the sale brings, okay?"

That night Phil's father, Pop, called. Deer hunting season started in four days and Pop and Phil's uncle Lucien, an attorney, were arriving two days early.

The next evening the four of us sat around the ranch kitchen dinner table, stuffing our mouths with my mashed potatoes and Lucien's meatloaf. "Son," said Pop. "Lucien and I are going with you to the auction. I'm curious about who bids and the amount they bid."

"Why, Dad?" asked Phil. "Are you interested in the ranch?"

"Yes, if I can purchase the redemption rights from the estate," he said. "I might be able to redeem if the auction price is low enough. I'll have to consolidate my other holdings, and see how much my house is worth. Then I'll try to convince your mother. She's dead set against selling our retirement properties and putting the money into the ranch."

"If it works out," said Lucien, "Jack's lifelong dream of owning a cattle ranch could come true."

After dessert, Phil's dad asked about the ranch's possibilities, like leasing pasture, putting up hay, buying hay, purchasing and selling the cows, doctoring and feeding the cowherd in winter. Phil and I tried to answer his questions as well as we could with our limited experience.

"Pop, it's incredible how much we learn just watching ranchers work," said Phil. "We ask them so many questions it's surprising they don't get new phone numbers, although, since it's a party line the neighbors hear everything anyhow."

"So there's much more to ranching than meets the eye," said Phil's father. "Is that what you're saying, son?"

"Yep."

The next morning the clouds pushed close to the earth. It hinted of rain. The four of us arrived at the courthouse a half hour early and saw some of our neighbors, the Hoffsteds, Gallaghers, Sloans, and Sheehans. In addition, two wealthy absentee Izee ranch owners whose land bordered Dad's, Gunter Nilsson and Damon Jacob, were present. People chatted in groups of threes and fours on the concrete steps of the stone courthouse in Canyon City. Sprinkled among them were strangers, whispering shared

3

conspiracies. Most likely attorneys. Their words hung in the air as we passed close.

"Mr. Timm died only two and a half *weeks* ago."

"What will happen to his daughter?"

"Well, she can't afford to buy the ranch, she—"

"Shush! That's her."

Our group sauntered towards Angus Sheehan's family. My ears rotated back trying to hear more gossip. While Angus, John, Gwen, Pop, Lucien, and Phil small-talked, my brain flooded with scrapbooky emotions. Gwen saw me struggling with melancholy so she caught my arm and pulled me aside. Grabbing both of my hands, she placed them on her stomach.

"Feel anything?" she said. "I'm pregnant. Due in March."

I hugged her, knowing that for a few years now she and John had hoped for a child.

"Gwen!" I said. "At least one good thing will come from this day, huh?"

A loud shout interrupted us.

"OKAY FOLKS!" yelled Sheriff Stone. "Let's start the bidding. What's my first bid on Paul Timm's ranch?" Sheriff Garner Stone, with his shaved head and compact frame, had a lawman's no-nonsense demeanor. The first to step up was Don Jones, the elderly cowman and original owner of dad's ranch.

"I bid $155,000.00 including the lien," Don said. Next to me, Pop mumbled, "That's good. Very good. Jones bid only the amount Paul owed him plus the judgment."

"SHERIFF!" All eyes turned to Damon Jacob. The Gallagher family managed his property. "I BID $175,000.00," Damon shouted. Shane Gallagher, his wife Anne, and Jeff stood next to Damon.

Then everyone looked at Gunter Nillson — and a hush fell over the crowd. The air was thick with expectation. People waited for his bid. No one spoke for three minutes. Would the two millionaires bid against one another?

"Anyone else? LAST CHANCE," said the sheriff. "The bid goes to Mr. Jacob."

Around us, a growing murmur rose above the watery burbling of Canyon Creek. Individual clusters of people leaned into each other chatting. Phil, Lucien, and Pop huddled. Later, I found out what caused the commotion. Other ranchers would have come prepared to bid if they'd known how low the bid would go. Lucky for us they didn't, because the

4

price could have risen too high.

So, we still had a home—for six months, anyway.

Three or four months had passed when Rafe stopped by with an offer to purchase the redemption rights by Gunter Nillson—who wanted to expand his holdings. Rafe, Gunter's ranch manager, representing his boss, offered us the 160 acres around our house, plus $15,000.

A week later two men, both strangers, came by our home and made a similar offer giving us 160 acres plus cash. We turned down this proposal because we'd already committed ourselves to Phil's father. At this point, Mike Jennings realized the estate couldn't just sell the redemption rights to Pop, so Mike set a date for the bids to be submitted.

As time sped by, suddenly the bidding deadline arrived. Damon Jacob's lawyer and the two strangers appeared at Mike Jenning's office right before five o'clock, the closing of the business day. Three bids were turned in and all bids were sealed. Mike opened each bid and Pop's bid was the highest. The ranch stayed in the family and we didn't have to move away. Pop got a loan for the rest of the purchase price and, to make the payments, he leased the ranch to an Izee neighbor, Ernst Hoffsted. After ten years, Phil convinced his dad to buy ten pregnant cows to build our herd and run the ranch ourselves.

It's been thirty-two years. We went from liberal hippies to conservative ranchers. Horseback riding still scares me but I've done a lot of it. Phil likes riding, thank God, because it is part of his job. I thrive in wide-open spaces, where my closest neighbor is a mile away, where the elk grazes on the hay meadow, the cougar passes in the night, a cow moos for her lost calf, and the coyotes sing us to sleep. . .In Izee. My home.

೫೫೫

FRIENDS THROUGHOUT THE YEARS

It is one of the blessings of old friends that you can afford to be stupid with them.

~Emerson

The Ladies

I still hear her voice on the phone, high and sweet. "Hi, friend. It's so good to talk to you. Shall we meet for lunch?"

Two months later, she was gone. Lark, still beautiful at eighty-one years young, walked into the fast flowing river next to her home during the ice-cold spring runoff. Her remains showed up fifteen months later about seven miles downstream. They knew it was Lark because some of the bones had metal repairs screwed into sockets. In her lifetime, Lark couldn't avoid a few horse wrecks.

We were an unlikely pairing. The only clue as to why she called *me* her friend was our shared silliness. Our lunches stretched sometimes for two raucous hours because we didn't want them to end. We wondered if the owner let us stay a couple of times after closing just to hear our rowdy laughter. Each meeting boosted our spirits. She was sharp, well read and a contemporary thinker. Even after she had a stroke she outdid me with her lightning fast humor.

When I started writing, I thought an article about her would fit perfectly in *RANGE* magazine. Cowgirls of her caliber were rare so I wanted to document her. I called her up and pretty much begged her for an interview. Since she hadn't driven through Izee in decades and wanted to see the country, she caved in and came for dinner.

As she spoke of her life, our elk stew cooled in our bowls, forgotten. Lark had to remind me to write down her words or turn the cassette over because I lost myself in listening to her story. I took notes and recorded her to remember what she said and, more important, to hear the way she said it. I sent her a draft to make sure she approved before submitting it to *RANGE*. I gave her all the notes and cassettes. When the article came out a few months later, she didn't hold back.

"Kristy," she told me, "people said you mixed up my words."

"Lark, you read it," I said. "Do you feel that way?"

"No," she said. "I liked it. Except for the photos. Kept thinking, who's that old person? Don't like looking at myself. Anyhow, don't know why the story struck some the wrong way."

I knew why. She was a legend. People want their legends to live up to their own personal criterion; true or not. She fit *my* idea of a legend. Even dying like a legend. I sorely miss our wild lunches together.

***

Another day and time involved my friend Swoozie's pregnancy. Swooze and her husband Jake, friends from John Day, were expecting their first child in a month. She convinced me to shop with her for maternity clothes. A nice sales lady looked at my pregnant friend, grabbed bras that resembled parachutes and pointed us to a curtained dressing room.

"Swoozie," I told her, "I'm not going to be any help 'cause I'm an ex-hippie, remember? Never wear a bra. What's different about a nursing bra anyway?"

"You got me," she said. "Mom just told me I needed to get one. My breasts are like udders. I'll have to declare them as dependents on our taxes."

I peeked into the changing room. "Oh man," I said, "this room is smaller than a bathroom cubicle. I'll wait out here for you."

"Nooo, Kristy," she said. "You'll have to hook it for me."

In the corner was a tiny bench no bigger than a child's chair, but it still took up a quarter of the space. I sat down dutifully. When Swooze entered, the room filled up with her breasts and hugely pregnant belly. We managed to lift her shirt off over her head and get her bra off. Reflected in the mirror, her chest looked like two pillows with nipples. She slipped on the straps of the maternity bra and I hooked it and sat down.

"How do these cup fasteners work—?" she asked. She swung around for help and smacked me in the face with her boobs. My head whipped back, bounced off the wall and back, landing in between her breasts. She fell back from the impact and into the mirror then boomeranged back into my face, smothering me.

"SwoozeIcan'tbreathebackaway." Suddenly her chest started shaking, taking my head along with it.

"Swooze!What'swrong?Isthebabycoming? Isthebabycoming? Breathe Breathe! ShouldIboilwater?Ripupthecurtain?"

"Hahahahahahahh." She gasped for breath. "Hooooohahahahaha." Hic. Hic. Hic. "Oh no, now I have the hiccups! Kris, I have to pee!"

The sales lady peeked in while my head was trapped between Swooze's jiggling breasts. Her eyes popped and sent us off again into huge gales of laughter. Although, I could only manage a muffled chuckling.

***

Conversations with my friend, Amy, usually made no sense because we

8

paid little attention to each other, but in a comfortable way. This is the reason we were friends. On our health walks along the highway between our ranches, she often entered into her netherworld while I jabbered about the surrounding scenery.

"Amy," I said, pointing at the asphalt. "Look at this squished mouse. It's folded in on itself." I bent down, my nose inches from the dead critter; I heard humming behind me. Her dreamy expression told me that at the moment she was Baryshnikov's ballet partner. The day-dreamy stuff happened when her interest didn't engage in the present situation. Amy had entered her fantasy mode.

Once, during a baseball game at the Oyster Feed in Seneca, Amy strolled past the field when a foul ball hit her head, snapping it horizontal and then upright again. She didn't break her stride because she believed herself to be invisible. Same with the time at Seneca's Elementary School Christmas show. Amy sat in the audience. She was supposed to yell "Elvis!" as part of the play but did it at the wrong moment. As heads turned to look at the culprit, Amy had already left her body. Her husband, Jeff, leaned over and said, "You goofball." He got no response because Amy was in her secret place, likely noshing on tea and scones with the Queen of England.

She helped Jeff around the ranch. In the winter, she drove the pick-up, pulling the hay wagon with Jeff feeding off it, often tossing him to the ground because of her erratic driving.

He'd run and jump back on. "Amy!" he'd holler, as oldies played on the radio and she sang "Pretty Woman" with Roy Orbison: "Don't walk away . . .hey . . ." or some other song.

"For God's sake, watch where you're going—!" Jeff would yell.

But, one time, he said it too late. Amy drove into the deep bull wallow then gunned it, pitching Jeff off once more. It was a pattern they'd perfected over the years without serious harm done. In fact, friends and acquaintances often mentioned in conversations that Jeff could easily join the U.S. Olympic Gymnastic Team— his acrobatic skills were listed in the Izee Book of Remarkable Feats.

I firmly believe this way of livestock feeding between husbands and wives is an acquired trait shared by ranch women.

Whenever I called Amy, she answered her phone just like a Stepford wife. "Amy." I said. "It's Kristy," This was probably the three hundredth phone call I'd made to her since our first meeting in 1974.

9

"Yes?" She was a crocodile wrestler, a governess, a Supreme Court judge; only *not* Amy.

"It's me. *Kristy.*"

"Ummm?" she'd purr. "How may I help you?" It was like talking to a blank screen. She just wasn't there. At these times, I gave up because my friend, Amy, had disappeared. But that was okay.

***

My first friend in Izee, Gwen Sheehan, taught school in Maupin and grew up in Grizzly, Oregon on her family's farm. She met John Sheehan in college and after John's stint in the army, they married and she joined him on one of the largest ranches in Izee. Since Dad knew the Sheehan family from hunting their ranch for years, we naturally gravitated toward John and Gwen. She worked side by side with John, the Sheehans' only child. The couple made a great pair and we had fun times.

One of our semi-regular activities became a two-hour round trip to the drive-in movies in John Day. One trip involved my nephew, Wade. John and Gwen liked him and treated him like a little brother.

"What's it about?" Wade asked Phil. "Scary? Gory? Girls in bikinis?"

"Eskimos," Phil said. "That's what John said."

"So bears ripping up people? Eskimos fooling around?"

"I doubt that," I told him. "It would be embarrassing."

Later, after settling in to our slot at the theatre, the speaker hooked on the driver's window, the movie began. Gwen brought out homemade popcorn. From the first frame, the Eskimos mumbled stuff in another language.

"Subtitles!" moaned Wade. "I lost my glasses today. They fell out of my pocket when I chased our milk cow into the barn! Can someone read the words for me?"

Phil and I mumbled our yeses, not crazy about the idea.

The Eskimo guy and girl on the screen smiled and gestured toward the igloo entrance. "Hey baby," Phil read, "join me in my bachelor's pad? We can rub each other in places other than our noses."

"You fresh cod—I mean cad," I added in falsetto. "What makes you think I'm interested in you?"

"I rubbed my body with whale oil," John continued, "just for you."

A white guy came into the igloo.

"Take my wife," I said. "Please."

10

"Alright, alright," Wade said, munching buttery popcorn. "I know they aren't saying that." He laughed and we settled down to watch and translate the real stuff.

Comfortable and easy. A rare thing. It was always like that with John and Gwen.

♋♋♋

Nita and Chopper

"Want to drop in on Nita?" Wade asked on our way out of John Day after a grocery run. "You'll like her and her family."

"Nita who?"

"Nita Parson. A few months ago, Paul drove into Nita's driveway drunk," said Wade. "Nita's son, Luke, drove Paul home. I drove Luke back to John Day and we've been friends ever since. I've had dinner at their house loads of times. Nita always wants to fatten me up just like her chubby animals."

"Oh, and watch out for the parrot," he said. "Nita loves the little horror. Its name's Chopper. Watch your head and keep alert."

Sounded like we were undercover agents going to a terrorist's lair.

"A bird?" said Phil. "How bad can it be?"

Wade grinned and entered the house with us following. Inside, a quick visual sweep showed no bird. We did see a baby goat, two lambs, a tiny calf getting bottle fed by a little girl with red hair, nine or thirty cats, and a water buffalo or two. Well, maybe not the water buffaloes, but if they'd fit somewhere Nita would have them.

Burlap sacks sagged against the walls. Some were labeled as Poultry Feed, Dog and Cat Food, Dried Colostrum, and Seed for Exotic Birds. Dirty rubber boots and squished gloves lay heaped near front and back doors. On top of one pile was an old-fashioned fur hand muff. When the doorbell rang behind us, the muff awoke and barked. A toothless, thousand–year-old lapdog with no lips, bee-lined for the door while first bumping into Phil's shoe then bouncing off a chair leg.

"She's got cataracts," said an outdoorsy-looking woman rising from behind a counter. Nita Parson's Mona Lisa smile welcomed us. The doorbell kept ringing.

"COME IN, DAMMIT!" she screamed at the door. All three of us jumped. "It's just Skeeter and Martha. Skeeter knows the damn door isn't locked, but he is forever ringing that shitty bell just to aggravate me. I swear I'll take a chainsaw to it someday." Then more ringing, as if some deranged doorbell-ringing serial killer wanted in.

"Did you hear the doorbell, Nita?" asked a young man with impish

12

eyes, a grin Shakespeare's Puck would envy, and a cowlick saluting the ceiling. "Wanted to be sure you heard us."

"Course I heard ya!" Nita scowled. "THE DEVIL IN HELL HEARD YA! AND SHUT THE DOOR OR CHOPPER WILL GET OUT!"

"Hi, Mom," said a pretty young woman trailing behind the man. A fat Gerber baby on her hip. She spotted us cowering in the corner. "I'm Martha. Skeeter loves bugging Mom."

"Hiya," Skeeter said, holding out his hand when, at the same time, the prehistoric dog returned and passed thunderous gas at our feet, causing it to spring up and bark at its bottom.

"Sounds just like Martha," said Skeeter. "Never knew girls farted until I met Martha." With that, Skeeter and Martha laughed so hard the effort proved Skeeter right, bringing additional gales of giggles, this time by everyone including someone behind us.

"Hi! I haven't cleaned my room in a year!" the tall toothpick bellowed two inches from our faces, causing us to close our eyes in defense. A toothy grin peered out of a curly flaxen mop. He disappeared through a door as fast as he'd materialized.

I glanced at Wade.

"Luke?"

"No, that was my youngest boy, Rollie," said Nita. "Luke and his dad are finishing a construction job in Susanville."

Introductions began, along with god-awful screeching. The raucous sound became background clamor but the family shouted over it. As we sat on a couch layered with The Real Mother Earth magazines, a small chartreuse blur whizzed by, landing on the back of the couch. Closer examination exposed what was thought to be an unusual design of the couch was instead layered bird dung, fresh and dried. The feathered perpetrator sat atop it like Tolkein's *Smaug* on his hoard of gold. The curtains hung in shreds which, oddly, had a sort of style. They were decorated with tiny greasy pellets of bird droppings.

"Wade's told us about you two," Nita said, ignoring Chopper's shrieking. "Would you like some fresh herb bread? Coffee? You two take it barefoot?"

"Uh, I better leave mine on if it's okay," I said, eyeing her floor with its crunchy bits. "I haven't trimmed my toenails in a while."

"Me, too," Phil added. "My socks have holes."

"No kids," she said, grinning. "I meant do you take anything in your coffee?" We shook our heads and she left for the kitchen.

Soon she placed coffee and herb bread near us, after she'd swept off a

13

mound of stuff onto the floor then retreated into another room. Seconds later and without warning, Chopper dove at us with the fearlessness of a Blue Angel; if the Blue Angels were green.

"Incoming!" Wade whispered. In tandem, we looked up as Chopper skimmed our noses in an avian drive-by. Vigorous arm waving and air slapping ensued as the parrot flew a Baron Von Richtoven zigzag between us. We gave each other a few friendly-fire wounds in the skirmish, but Chopper escaped unharmed.

"Wade," whispered Skeeter, "the flyswatter." Skeeter flung it; Wade caught it in mid-air just as Chopper started a second attack. Wade assumed a batter stance when suddenly Nita returned. Wade, with a style rivaling Baryshnikov's, pirouetted, turning the whack into a reenactment of a sneak-up-on-a-deer hunt. I, for one, never knew Wade was so limber and graceful.

"Then I jumped behind the sage bush before the 5-point spotted me." Chopper also used Wade's hunter's ballet to dive straight onto Phil's unprotected coffee cup, giving new meaning to Nita's question of wanting anything in our coffee. The amber brew splashed all over Phil's shirt. Unfazed, Chopper climbed out, shook, took off and disappeared.

"Look at that," said Nita, tickled at her parrot's antics. "Isn't he clever?"

Phil, trying not to sputter, asked if he could use the bathroom. Nita pointed to a door. Wade and Martha started a coughing fit. After Phil entered and shut the door, Skeeter leaned against the wall near the bathroom, smiling.

"Ahhhhh! Get away from me!"

Phil's yells caused Skeeter to move closer to the door. Inside the bathroom, muffled thumps and banging rivaled Gene Krupa's famous drum solos.

"STOP IT! I'M WARNING YOU! Okay. That's it!"

THWACK! The door opened. Phil stood there, hair wild. From behind him, Chopper soared out, dropping a poop on Phil's collar with the accuracy of a Michael Jordon jump shot.

We made excuses for a speedy departure; something like Phil suffers from a condition similar to Tourette's Syndrome, where he can't help acting crazy when he goes into other people's bathrooms. It's a childhood thing, we said. Doctors don't know what to call it, but he has to go home and take his medicine. The puzzled look on Nita's face told us that maybe she worried Phil's condition was catching. Or that we were idiots. So much for first impressions.

In the car, heading home, Phil gave us the story on the bathroom episode:

"I was standing there, you know, and had already started when Chopper landed on the back of the toilet," he said, his voice shaky. "I thought, surely he would stay put. Then without warning, he flew straight at my face. It was like when the birds attacked Tippi Hedren in the attic in Hitchcock's movie, *The Birds*. I couldn't stop going. I sprayed everywhere: walls, towels, the baby's binky — it was bad! I grabbed a towel and went after him. The more I struck near him, the faster he dodged. It was like I was teaching him how to duck and weave. He flew up high and landed. While keeping an eye on him, I did a quick scrub of the baby's binky and got out of there. It's the stuff movies are made of. Horror flicks. You know? Deranged bird trying to disfigure a person when they're helpless?" Phil babbled all the way home.

***

It was a month or two before Phil and I went back. The devil bird's behavior pretty well decided that, for Phil, a return visit to Nita's wouldn't happen unless, next time, he could squirt the wings of the flying antichrist with extra-hold hairspray. He nearly got his wish when Wade reported back to us after a visit to Nita's.

"It was a beautiful thing," Wade said. "Chopper walked across Nita's husband Charlie's plate of pancakes. That did it. If Nita hadn't threatened to leave Charlie, Chopper would be burning in bird hell, but instead she gave him to an elderly neighbor who has an aviary. Luke told me the guy says Chopper's quite *rambunctious*."

Bard Culpepper

Oh, heck! It must be Bard Culpepper, pulling into our driveway in a beat up, grumbly ranch rig, the irascible cowboy who worked at the ranch next door. His reputation painted him as gruff with a short fuse. As I peeked at him past the white cotton curtain of the window, he swung out of his doorless rattrap.

Well, I wasn't in the mood for his quick temper. He had better watch out, even if he did pack a pistol in a shoulder holster. Feeling sassy, I was out the door before he walked around the vehicle. With his frowning black eyebrows and huge handlebar mustache, he looked intimidating. He began gesturing wildly, cussing and arguing with some unseen adversary. Then he caught sight of me.

"Is yur husband here?" he said with a growl. "I need t' talk t' him. Right now." He shot me a steely glare with one eye squinted. My sense of humor kicked in as I watched Bard Culpepper turn into Yosemite Sam right before my eyes. Who could take a cartoon character seriously?

"Are we having a bad day, Mister Culpepper?"

A few heartbeats went by and I stood my ground with my nose as uppity as I could get it. Then I noticed what looked like two bullet holes in the side panel of his jeep. Slowly, his face softened and his eyes crinkled up.

"I shot the jeep," he said, pointing to the holes. "It wouldn't start so I got pissed off at it."

"You just shot it."

"Yup," he said, with a sheepish grin. "Wal, anyhow, tell Phil I stopped. Warn't nothing particular I wanted."

We mentally shook hands. I often attacked inanimate objects, too. Here was an ally — a soul akin to mine, with a sense of the ridiculous. It was the beginning of an enjoyable friendship, at least on our part.

Bard was prickly and cantankerous, but he was also an intelligent and talented cowman, moving up the ranks to ranch manager of the neighboring ranch. Hard work, helpfulness, integrity, and loyalty were his principles of life.

He was available to his neighbors anytime, anywhere. If we needed

16

help, he urged us to call, which was usually necessary as we built up our herd. At certain times of the year, like calving or branding, he never hung up on our semi-hysterical phone calls or said no to our cry for help. We wouldn't have blamed him for complaining to his wife for having those *! #/#!! needy greenhorns as neighbors.

Although, his generosity didn't make us immune to his trickster side. One of his pranks happened at the peak of our angst: Calving season.

Calving was still a new experience to us and fraught with emergencies. We'd drive through the herd examining each cow's rear end. Tight, swollen udders, a long bloody string hanging from the vagina, and round pouches on the vagina the ranchers call moccasins, were all possible signs of a calf birth.

One frosty morning we set out to feed as usual. I hopped out of the passenger's side of the red flatbed truck, and unlatched the barbed wire gate. I dragged it back, and spotted a small furry bundle lying still a few feet away. Alarms started banging in my brain: a dead calf. Phil jumped from the truck and we stood over the poor little bugger. It was not only dead but also horribly deformed. We felt like failures. What did we do wrong?

Heartsick, we finished throwing the hay off the truck. We chafed at our inexperience. We walked through the herd three times. Phil began wondering where the mother was and why she wasn't standing over the dead calf. There was no sign of a fresh calved cow without a baby. Its fur was dirty and matted, indicating a rough tongue hadn't cleaned it off. When Phil nudged it with his boot, it was rock hard. After a while, a question sprouted in our novice brains. What if the calf wasn't from our herd?

That possibility grew until, after lots of discussion, we decided that maybe we'd been had. Then we knew. *Culpepper*.

We also suspected that Bard anticipated the usual harried phone from us so we let him stew. Then a couple of weeks later, Bard and his hired man, Joaquin, stopped at our corrals where Phil was repairing the fence. Phil played the innocent.

"How's the calvin' goin'?" Bard asked. "Anything unusual bin happenin' t' speak of?" That infinitesimal eye twinkling showed in Bard's eyes. Phil knew that Bard was mining for information.

"Ya know," said Bard, sidling up to the subject. "We've had an unusual amount of odd happenins among our calves. Why, we've had sloughed calves, calves stomped by their muthers, and even a Lupine-caused deformity or two."

He shot Phil an intense glance. "How 'bout you?"

"No, nothing yet," Phil said, maintaining his normal casual, calm attitude. "I sure hope nothing goes wrong." He delivered the line as smooth as a seasoned stage veteran.

Bard thoughtfully twisted his left mustache tip, stared at Phil a minute, then left.

Days later, we pulled up to Bard's feed wagon lumbering down the highway and Phil fessed up that we'd figured out his subterfuge. He and Joaquin had already decided a coyote had dragged the deformed calf away and that's why we never said anything. It was a sweet victory and a rare one when dealing with Bard's practical jokes. Although *we* never reciprocated, Nature did. Bard foolishly provoked the arbitrary forces of earth, wind, and fire.

One spring season he wanted to burn some fields to get rid of the wolfy bunch grass, sage stands, and spiky dried thistles. A century-old, dilapidated barn of ours sat next to the meadow Bard planned to burn. Bard's Bic lighter and a cooperating wind started the flames traveling at a good clip away from our barn and fields.

But in a fraction of a second, the fickle breeze shifted, escalated, and leaped to the barn. Horrified, Bard flew to his truck to call on his CB.

"Janie!" he told his wife, in between gulps of air. "Call Phil t' help me. I've burnt 'is barn! The fire's movin' up Soda!"

Phil arrived as Bard ran all over the ground stomping out flames, his boots smoking. They hoe-downed hard for an hour until another wind shift turned the fire back onto itself.

One would think Bard had learned his lesson but he still had the fever. It might have to do with being lightning-struck a few times. After he burned our barn, he and Phil were repairing a mutual border fence. Bard parked at the meadow's edge. With a lengthy rope, he'd tied his new dog, Zuppy, to the pickup bed to keep him from getting into mischief while Bard was preoccupied.

Bard eyeballed the chunky tall rye next to the low cut grass of the hay meadow. He licked a stubby finger, held it in the air, and took out his Bic. By now, Phil had the bug too and nodded at Bard. Soon a proper line of flames overtook the woody stems. Satisfied at the fire's steady advancement, they tramped up the hill and into a gully to patch the fence. A half an hour later, their chore accomplished, they headed downhill. Reaching the rise, they were astonished to see that the fire's blackened path had followed the hill down and traveled directly under the truck.

Rubbing their eyes in disbelief, they hightailed it to the vehicle. Hunkered on top of the tire next to the fuel tank above the smoldering ground was Zuppy. Untouched. The dog, like Bard, went through several lifetimes in just a few seconds. Still, it would take more than a little thing like an exploding gas tank to diminish Bard's passion for scouring the land of ancient fuel-worthy flora.

The desire to rid the ranch of useless old grasses once again emerged and the picture of verdant green grass after a burn galvanized Bard. He leaped out of his truck near a formidable patch of dried weeds. The Bic appeared and performed its magic.

Underestimating the superior fuel material, Bard watched dumfounded as this fire whooshed and headed back towards his pickup. Then, as he came to his senses, Bard sprinted to it, arriving ahead of the fire. Inside, his happy dog, Winnie, jumped on the door pawing at the closed windows. Bard knew it before it happened; in slow motion, her paws came down.

Click.

Bard raced to the other door. So did his Winnie, playing the game. Before Bard reached the door, he realized his mistake. Winnie was already there.

Click.

He whipped around to face the fire.

Miraculously, and by the good graces of that other practical joker, Nature, Bard got a reprieve. The lapping flames obeyed the wind and turned away in anticipation of the next amusing rendezvous with Bard and his legendary Bic lighter.

ಎಎಎ

Izee Neighbors

In the mid-seventies, the community of Izee began changing. Multi-generational families had always lived on the ranches. Ranching was a hard lifestyle and occupation to maintain even for a single family, let alone two or three. Other things contributed: low cattle prices, expenses, the rising cost of hay, and young adults leaving for city jobs. Eventually all these things combined to take its toll.

Soon wealthy absentee owners or new ranching families started buying ranches. A massive property turnover occurred when generational ranches sold and families relocated all over the United States. Traditional neighboring in Izee suffered a setback until the new people got to know the Izee ranchers.

This is where we came in. Hippie/designer-craftsmen; we made our living designing and selling our work elsewhere. The ranch was our home— not our work. For years, the only people who lived in Izee were either owners or hired folks, all of whom worked the land and tended the animals. Often new blood was suspect. Maybe the upside to this was, well . . . new blood.

***

"Time to make lunch," I told Phil. "Peanut butter and grape jelly sandwiches coming up in fifteen." The lawn had a skiff of snow as I walked from the shop to the house. A gravel crunching noise made me glance toward the highway. There, walking down the road was one of the prettiest girls I have ever seen. She looked like an angel. I didn't see ethereal wing-ery on her but she could have tucked her wings in. Angels can do anything they want. Well, except defy God. That's a huge no-no. Just ask Satan, right? Anyhow, her hair was spun white-gold like the fairy princesses in *Grimm's Fairy Tales*. Or, Goldberry in *Lord of the Rings*.

"Oh hi," she said, smiling Shirley Temple dimples. "I'm Sally. My in-laws just bought the ranch next to yours. Cam and June Johnson? I'm married to their son, Lance."

"Wow," I told her. "We don't see beauteous girls strolling down the highway often. I thought you were a lost angel or something." She laughed a great laugh.

"Hahaha!" she said, "I'm hardly an angel!"

I wasn't convinced. Angels visit people all the time in disguises. Although, I couldn't see the reason for an angelic visit on our road. Unless Phil or I were in need of some help we didn't know about. A test was what was called for in this situation.

"Neat country, huh?" I gently baited as I walked nearer. "Look! Up on the hill across the road. Gosh! Is that a Bald Eagle?" She turned around to look and I closely examined her back for any signs of wing humps, or shiny feather parts sticking out from a sleeve or collar. Nothing. I had one more idea as she turned back around.

I grabbed her. "Well, for heavens sake! Give me a hug! That's what we do here is hug newcomers!" I said, moving my hands around on her back. "You sure feel cold. Let me rub you a bit to get that circulation going again."

"Um . . . uh . . ." she tried to communicate to me, but I had her mouth snuggled tight into my armpit. My hugs are well-known for their magnitude.

"Mufity eyelif shorigee," she mumbled. "Buxher!"

"That's angel talk, right?" I asked as I released her. "Gee, somehow I thought it would be more musical." She backed up, her demeanor now panicky.

"Is everyone out here like you?"

"Pretty much," I fibbed. "Izee is a friendly bunch of folks."

"I have to go leave now." She turned and *ran* home. I got a good look at her retreating back and—nothing.

"Okay!" I yelled at her. "Bye for now! Looking forward to you teaching me heaven talk!"

***

That same ranch went through four owners within a span of ten or fifteen years and, in the spirit of neighborliness, unless it was during hunting or haying season, the community gave a welcoming party for new folks. We attended the party for Hank and Bo Stratton. The Gallagher family hosted it at their house. They asked everyone to bring finger food, so I whipped up some cookies shaped and decorated like fingers and thumbs; complete with fingernails.

As I stood holding my plate full of starch-ridden potluck food (my favorite), I noticed Mrs. Stratton sitting on the couch all alone. I headed over. I passed by Cam Johnson visiting with Noel Gallagher, who had a finger cookie paused to take a bite and oddly, the finger looked like it was getting ready to pick his nose. *Jeez, maybe my cookies are inappropriate. Nah.*

21

"Hi, Mrs. Stratton!" I said. "I'm Kristy St. Clair and we border you to the east, west, and south. Gee, that almost sounds like a musical with John Raitt and Jane Powell doesn't it? Like *Oklahoma!* Hahaha." I sat down on the old lumpy couch next to her. She bounced up when I sat down. My bottom nearly touched the floor and I ended up with my chin on my knees. Plates of food, napkins, and plastic forks were barely saved.

"Welcome to Izee," I said. "You're from New Mexico?" She smiled and nodded. A cookie digit rested on her full plate.

"Nice to meet you, Kristy," she said. "Yes, we're from Santa Fe and, boy, it's a lot colder here than I thought it would be. Um . . . who do you suppose made these strange cookies?"

"Beats me," I said, quickly changing the subject. "Yes, it's cold but so lovely. The desert, creeks, river, and the beautiful hills!" I gushed, using my hands as an exclamation point. "I— absolutely — love— it!" On the downhill gesture, my hand hit my plastic fork loaded with potato salad, sending it in a high loop and landing it perfectly in Bo's plate of barely touched carbohydrates. Potato salad intact. Out of the corner of my eye, I saw amused faces look away. Bo's expression remained composed.

"Not in a million years could you do that again," she said, eyes twinkling. "Well done."

I smiled back. "I made the cookies."

***

Oddly, brandings were also a good way to welcome newcomers into the fold. Young and old were given jobs based on safety, skill level, and degree of squeamishness. That's probably why I always got the testicle container job — normally given to children. Kids usually watched avidly when the rancher did the testicle cutting, but I stared at anything but the knife action and tried to think about Mary Poppins or the Scarecrow in Wizard of Oz. Happy thoughts, happy thoughts. My neighbors probably preferred the children's help and I can't blame them.

***

All in all, the Izee community, even during population shifts, welcomed new folks, young and old. The new people found diversity here, and contributed their own. The glue to this was, and is, that we all learned to neighbor one another. Mostly because we are all we have, and like a blood-related family, we have no choice. And that's not a bad thing.

ᏚᏚᏚᏚ

Izee Kids

While we were visiting the Sweets, Joel squirmed his way onto my cushiony chair. There was room enough for only one adult and one kid. The four-year-old stared at his lap and at mine, snuggled side by side. He looked up at me then down at our laps a couple more times, a puzzled look on his face.

"We're sitting together?" he said, amazed. "You've got a tiny butt." Martha heard him and burst out laughing.

"It's 'cause your mama's too fat, son," she said, grinning. "Is that it?"

"Yes!" Joel said, "You're too fat!"

The whole family started laughing, cracking themselves up. Phil and I fidgeted, not used to their frankness.

"No," I told her. "You're *Rubenesque.*" That set off a new gale of hilarity.

"Kristy," said Skeeter, her husband. "Martha's fat. You can say it." Martha nodded, a big smile on her face. No, I couldn't say it. Wouldn't say it. She was a beautiful woman.

"It's okay," she said, her smile sweet. "It doesn't hurt my feelings."

While everyone was busy chuckling, Matt, the Sweet's two-year-old son tried to climb up too.

"Nooo, Matt. Stay off. I'm up here. Stay down! We don't want you." Joel kept pushing his little brother down. Pretty soon the boys scuffled and shoved each other.

"BOYS!!" screamed Martha, smiling as she said, "Little shits," but not meaning it one bit. They were jewels — a couple of the best kids Phil and I knew. In fact, we actually wished we had our own after being around these lovable little guys. So when Skeeter and Martha asked if we could keep them for a couple of days while she had their third child, we were honored, but terrified and clueless.

Shouldn't have worried, the boys told us what to do, how to dress them, what to feed them, what time to put them to bed. It's like they had sympathy for the pitiable adults their folks left them with. All went smoothly for the two days we had them. The third day was church day and then back to their folks.

Sunday morning, Skeeter called from the hospital. The boys could come home after church and see their new baby sister. But first, bath time. It seemed easier and faster to sponge bathe the boys.

"Okay, Joel, I'll start with you. Take off your clothes because I need to clean you with a wash cloth." Both boys looked at me like I was a demon from hell.

"It'll be all right guys. See? I'll just run this wet, soapy wash cloth up and down your arms and legs and stomach and such." I was busy with the job when a somber baritone broke through my thoughts.

"Don't wash my butt."

"What, honey?"

"Don't wash my butt."

"Oh! Okay."

"Mine neither!"

"Okay, boys. Don't worry," I said. A giggle tried to bubble up but I squelched it. Bad time for humor—these two boys were dead serious. "All done! Let's get your church clothes on!"

While they dressed themselves with little help from me, I decided they were too young to notice if I dressed in front of them. It would allow me the chance to keep an eye on them, too.

As I stepped out of my robe, Matt wandered over to the bed, looking at something. He looked at me (now shirtless) then again at the bed.

"Is this your tiny bra?" Matt asked, holding my bra in his hands. He pointed at my chest. "Are those your tiny boobs?"

***

Country kids are as involved in cow work as their parents. One evening during calving season, we called our neighbor, Jeff Gallagher, to look at our heifer.

Jeff and his two kids, Shelly and Sage, hopped out of the Chevy pickup just as Phil got our heifer in the head catch.

"Where's the fire, Phil?" Jeff said, smiling as he walked up to the chute. "Or maybe a tornado from the sound of your voice on the phone."

"Thanks for coming, Jeff. Hi kids," Phil said. "My heifer has calved and now she has a uterine prolapse that looks like half of her insides are sticking out of her bottom."

"Boy," said Jeff, "you aren't kiddin'. Except it looks more like a girl I used to date. Only prettier." His sixteen-year-old daughter, Shelly, chuckled and swatted him.

"Put a wig on it and no one could tell the difference," Jeff said. "Okay. Enough silliness. Shelly, go get my pistol." Phil paled. "No, I'm only *joshin'* Phil. Shelly, hon, can you go get my tackle box out of the truck? Make sure the needles, surgical tape, boluses, antiseptic, and needle gun are in there before you bring it? Thanks, honey. Oh, and the big thermos, too."

Jeff arranged his equipment neatly on a crooked old desk we had in the corral for this purpose. Shelly stuck the needle tip of the needle gun into a bottle of LA-200, an antibiotic, and drew the amber liquid down until it showed 25 cc. Sage then threaded a foot of surgical tape into the eye of a single three-inch arched needle, leaving about a foot and a half trailing. Phil took a few boluses out of the box so they'd be available. Jeff poured on antiseptic then warm water from the thermos all over the engorged area to clean it.

"Okay now, son," said Jeff. "Stand behind the cow, put both hands on the prolapse, and push hard." The ten-year-old boy looked at the sticky, dripping, bloody calving bed then at his dad. Involuntary gulping, burpy noises erupted from Sage. His stomach heaved and gurgled and his mouth worked like a grouper.

"What's the matter?" said Jeff. "Prolapse got your tongue?" Sage grinned, while his dad chuckled but the boy still urped out a few more sounds.

"Well, let . . . us . . . proceed!" Jeff said. "We've got work to do. And now I'm serious."

He and Phil both gathered the blood-filled, spongy mass and started slowly working it into the heifer. The cow reacted with a contraction and it oozed out again. She was done with the thing and wasn't taking it back. A half hour crawled by and the sun set.

"Oh jeez!" Jeff grunted. "Are we stuffing it into right hole?" Phil bent over, his nose almost touching the stuffed-in place.

"It's too dark to tell but it feels smaller than before."

"Sage," Jeff yelled, slightly panicky, "go grab a flashlight from the truck." In a flash the boy returned and shined the beam into his dad's eyes. "Not in my eyes, son. On the cow's rear end!"

Then the light leaped over to Phil's eyes. "I can't see! I can't see! Now I know how a mole feels," Phil said, "only we don't have their big teeth."

Sage finally lit up the prolapse. Their vision returned and Jeff and Phil saw that it was going into the right place.

"I once knew a guy," Jeff said, "who worked for forty-five minutes on a prolapse only to discover he'd stuffed most of it into the bung-hole."

Sage and Shelly got the giggles just thinking about it.

25

Another fifteen minutes of pushing passed and suddenly the blob disappeared inside the cow. Phil, Jeff, and the kids started whooping and hollering, briefly forgetting the prolapse.

"Dad! Look!"

Sure enough the mass started reappearing. Closest, Jeff laid hands on it in time and pushed it back in. Phil, grabbing the opportunity, stuffed a few boluses inside.

"Now Shelly, you have the smallest hands, so you hold the prolapse in while I stitch it up around you. Sage, bring me the needle and string." Jeff poked the needle through the thick lips and began making crisscross stitches that looked like the laces on a tennis shoe, but looser so the cow could still go to the bathroom. Shelly's bubblegum pink nail polish gleamed in contrast to the red mass she was holding in. Jeff tied off the stitching with a square knot.

"There now," Jeff said. "You can let go, honey. Phil, go ahead and give her a total of thirty ccs of L.A., intramuscular, but don't put it all in one spot."

"Dad," said Shelly, "can we go now? I still have to get ready for the prom tonight."

"Oh, by golly, I almost forgot!" Jeff said. "It'll give me enough time to clean my shotgun before —what's his name again?"

"Dad! You know it's Jake!"

"Oh yeah," said Jeff. "Well, it doesn't matter if he's the football hero at school, he's still the kid who will face my gun if he doesn't get my daughter home before his rattrap of a car turns into a pumpkin! Are you gonna tell him that just a couple of hours ago you were playing with a cow's privates? "

"Dad!"

ରେରେରେ

OUR DADS

Two men, so different, yet they shared humor, love of life,
and a deep regard for their families...

Dad and the First Ranch

Dad had a history of unique situations concerning friends, family, food, and critters. As a kid he was my hero, and we went everywhere together. As a teen I lost faith in my dad because of his behavior. For a parent, it must be a horrendous thing to see your status change in your child's eyes. Even so, I loved him and didn't realize what *I'd* lost until he was gone. But the memories remain. Here are a few of the best of them.

In Orland, California, 1957, we lived on another ranch. The house was a mansion with three floors, maid's room and stairway, high ceilings, two massive fireplaces, and lots of empty rooms. Groves of olives, pomegranates, lemons, cherries, almonds, and apples lined the long driveway in. Sheep and horses grazed in lush grass pastures. Dad taught me to swim in the huge swimming pool in the back yard. My dad always took me with him, even to the corrals, where I perched on the top pole watching Dad while he and the hired hands worked the sheep. "Honey, stay on the fence until the sheep go by," Dad said. "Be quiet and still, okay?"

My view from the top pole showed the sheep below going into a smelly bath and out again to the corral. The hands and Dad hustled the sheep quickly through. Sometimes one escaped, then all hell erupted, and Dad reverted to his second language.

"Get that g** damn sheep!" he yelled. "The piece of s*** needs to get the hell out of there, now!"

Mom walked up behind me as I yelled (like my hero just did), "Yeah, get that g**damn sheep!!"

"Kristy," Mom said. "Stop that!" I was puzzled. *Dad* got to say that, so what's the problem?

He joined us after the big sheep escape was over.

"Mr. Timm," Mom said. "Kristy just cussed. Where did she hear that kind of talk?"

"G**Dammit, Dart, how the hell should I know?"

Later, long after lunch, Dad stood over the freezer and motioned me over. "Honey," he whispered, "Want a piece of chocolate?" From the frozen depths, Dad brought out a block of milk chocolate the size of a Webster's dictionary. He sat it on the washer lid, took a hammer, and came down hard on the icy confection. Four or five pieces of chocolatey morsels broke off and he handed me two. We stood enjoying the blissfulness of chocolate when something occurred to me.

"Why did you whisper, Daddy?"

"Because it makes the chocolate taste better, don't you think? Plus, it's like an adventure movie. The evil bad guy doesn't know that we have a secret stash of chocolate or that it gives us super human strength to fight off evil, like Superman."

He convinced me. The whole time we lived there, we'd share hunks of chocolate every night—just the two of us. To this day, it's the only reason I eat lots of chocolate: to fight off evil. I'm pretty sure that's why we've never been attacked by scary nether-world things.

Then there were the frog legs. In Orland, frog hunting was big. At night people went out to the marshy areas, speared frogs, brought them home, cut the legs off, and fried them up. Frog legs were a delicacy in that area of Northern California. Everyone loved fried frog legs, except me. They were creepy and, after they're cut from the body, the legs still wiggled. I preferred the frog alive and whole and hopping in its marsh or where I could watch it live on its jumping legs with them still attached. They were also in that freezer. I saw them. They lay there like frog ice lollies next to the chocolate block. When I found out what they were, I didn't want the chocolate either. Dad noticed and hid them under packages of beef, lamb, and venison, so the shared chocolate munching time returned sans frog popsicles.

The Orland ranch also had some dandy bird hunting. Dad liked to hunt all the edible game birds. He had me run through a corn field to scare up the pheasants.

"Kristy, honey," he said, "we'll start walking, you in front of me, and when I yell, RUN, you take off shouting through the corn."

Dad closed his shotgun and lifted it to his shoulder. "RUN!"

I took off running and screaming. In front of me big, beautiful pheasants rose up from the corn.

BOOM, BOOM, BOOM! The shotgun went off behind me. Three birds folded their wings and fell to the earth.

"Thank you, princess," he said. "Looks like you and your grandfather's gun got us some beauts. Let's go fry 'em up, okay? Nothing tastes as good as corn-fed pheasants." He smacked his lips. "You did a wonderful job, honey." As corny (okay, cheap shot) as it sounds, *any* food tasted good when I was with Dad.

Dad went goose and duck hunting, too, on marshes behind the ranch house. I was stuck in school and identified moodily with Tom Sawyer and Huck Finn minus the gruesome, murdering Injun Joe. This time it was goose season, at early dawn with Dad's friend Dutch, a hulk of a man.

Dutch had a nifty blind in a marsh behind his property adjoining ours. His old Touring canoe barely held both men, who were over six feet tall. They placed it behind the heavy marsh grasses and phony grass in front of the blind. The decoys floated out thirty feet away. Dutch blew his special goose call. An answering call came from above. Suddenly four geese floated down and both men shouldered their guns and shot. Two geese fell close, so Dad reached around the blind, grabbed their necks and brought them into the boat.

"That just never happens, man!" said Dutch. "What were the odds on that, huh? Falling almost at our feet! That's the way to hunt!" Dad agreed, taking a sip from the offered whiskey flask.

"Think we scared off the rest?" asked Dad. "Hope not. Let's stay a little longer."

Dutch laid the geese next to him under the aft point. Both men opened their shotguns, reloaded, and stared out at the water, waiting.

A rustling made Dutch turn. Staring face to face with him was one of the geese.

"AAAAHHH," they yelled. "Grab it!" gasped Dutch. Dad grabbed its neck and wrestled it, finally getting it down after a five- minute battle.

"What the HELL . . .?" said Dad, panting. "Didn't know they were that strong!"

"Me neither," Dutch added. "Likely to scare the pants off me!" Out came the flask and more chugging. Both guys hands shook.

"Try again?" Dutch asked Dad.

"Hell, yeah," he said. "I still hear more geese up there."

"One more?" Dutch said, holding up the flask.

"You betcha!" said Dad, "nectar of the gods!" The flask was tipped and they gulped some healthy swallows.

Dutch felt the hair on his neck rise. He turned and once again the goose's long neck rose like a Phoenix from the fire and pointed its beak straight at Dutch's face.

"Ah! Ah! Ah! Ahhhhhh!" he yelled, backing into my dad. "It's back. It can't be killed by man! Save yourself!"

30

Dad caught the neck and battled madly with the Canadian goose.

"It's like rassling a full-on fire hose!" Dad gasped. "Grab its body, Dutch."

"No!" yelled Dutch. "I can't—I won't. He'll, he'll kill me! I just know it!"

"Hah! He's down!" said Dad. "SHOOT IT. SHOOT IT."

"Here? It's too close! We'll be maimed—"

"NOW!"

KABLAM!

"Good God, man," said Dad. "How'd you miss me?"

"Don't know, but the goose went the way of the Wicked Witch of the West, minus the ruby slippers."

On another excursion into the Orland ranch bird-hunting realm, Dad and Uncle Ralph got up early to bag some ducks. The night before there was a stag party for Uncle Ralph's son-in-law. Too much imbibing left them with hangovers, and the autumn air could freeze off a duck's bill. But they were determined to continue their plans to duck hunt that day.

They drove out to a jetty and parked.

Since Dad was a crack shot, they decided Uncle Ralph would walk around and then crawl into the swamp behind the unsuspecting birds and scare them toward Dad.

"It'll take you about a half hour to get around them," Dad said. "When you hear me shoot, come back." Dad stood and watched Uncle Ralph walk around the marshy lake. Dad's eyelids kept shutting, so he got back in the warm car. *I'll just take a quick nap*, he thought.

Forty-five minutes later, somebody pounded on the driver's side window. Dad, startled, woke up and saw the visage of Uncle Ralph, mud-caked and dripping with marsh grass crisscrossing his face.

"I waited for an hour in the freezing air!" screamed Uncle Ralph, red-faced, blue lipped, and raging. "Let me in, you bastard!" He pounded and pushed, shaking the car.

"Not until you calm down, Ralph."

"LET ME IN OR ELSE!!!"

Dad looked at him and locked the doors.

ഗഗഗ

31

Drunk in Reno

Dad was drunk in Reno. His bull-buying trip had turned into a week-long bender. To make matters worse, Grant County had slapped a lien on the ranch for failure to spray for noxious weeds, and Dad's court appearance was two days away. Someone needed to go get him.

The hotel manager, Buster, an old friend of my parents, contacted my mother. She couldn't get off work to travel, so she called me.

"Honey," she told me, "Buster's confined your dad to his room, with bodyguards to keep him out of trouble. A hooker rolled him for fifteen thousand dollars he'd won at the tables. He's escaped twice looking for a drink, but they caught him before he got into the casino. The switchboard operators stopped his outgoing calls." She drew a breath. "Sweetheart, can you go?"

Oh shoot. Wouldn't want to miss a fun rescue trip to Reno. It was a brief, ungrateful-child moment.

"Sure, Mom."

Phil wasn't happy but didn't want me going alone. So the next morning, Wade drove us to the airport in Redmond, Oregon. Mom had arranged for three tickets. We'd get Dad and return the same day.

At the hotel in Reno, Buster's two strapping bodyguards answered our knock, smiling as they let us into Dad's room. Dad looked like an old vampire, except he had a Maalox mustache, while vampires have blood mustaches. Although they both lounge around in bathrobes.

"Dad, the ranch has a problem only you can fix, so we've come to take you home," I said, stuffing his clothes into his suitcase. "Can you get dressed? We're flying back to the ranch in a couple of hours."

"Okay," he said, jumping up. "I'll just get a quick drink."

Phil motioned to me. "Kristy," he said, in a voice louder than usual, "Would you join me, please?" Grabbing my arm, he hustled me into the cramped bathroom.

"Phil, wouldn't you prefer to be by yourself in here?"

"Listen, the airlines won't let him fly in this condition," he said, whispering. "Look at him!"

Dad, now talking to a guard, gestured wildly, talked loudly, scratched himself everywhere, and ignored his runny nose.

"What do we do," I said, "short of thunking him on the head?"

But as I said that, I thought of old movies. Somebody always slipped a mickey into the drink of an unsuspecting victim to knock them out. Surely, all Nevada casino hotels had mickeys or knockout drops stashed discreetly behind the bar or tucked away in a secret, locked drawer for situations such as this.

"C'mon," I said. Phil followed. Trusting. Clueless.

Downstairs in the casino, the pit boss resembled a burly James Cagney. A jaded expression flashed across his scowling face. His dark suspicious eyes inched over my scrawny frame, taking in the blonde braids, worn jeans, and fitted western shirt. They finally rested on the scratched, dusty cowboy boots standing on his fancy red carpet.

"This casino ain't got no mickeys," he said, "and it's healthier if you didn't ask questions like that, girlie." His junkyard-dog pose shifted, projecting a *get-outta-here-now* move.

Dazzling insults about his family tree having no branches simmered deep in my throat, but Phil, the wisest of our union, dragged me away. "Why didn't you fill me in about your pending death-by-hit-man idea?" he said, gasping. "I could have called my parents to say goodbye first. Kristy, we're in *The Godfather* movie."

Phil yammered at me all the way back to Dad's room. Behind the door, we heard shouting. We knocked.

"Don't you know who I am?" my father roared at the bodyguards like God to Moses. "I own a *four-thousand* acre cattle ranch!" he said. "I'll let you work for me and be a cowboy, if you get me get a drink."

The two bodyguards, ignoring Dad's outburst, let us back in the room. One leaned against the door while the other sat down and pulled out a dog-eared paperback from his back pocket titled *Passion on the Moors*. Boy, I thought, Dad had barked up the wrong tree with that guy.

Dad dropped dramatically onto the rumpled bed, sulking and scheming, while Phil and I sat in the corner, still trying to figure a way to get my father onto the plane. That's when Dad suddenly grabbed his phone.

"Room service?" he asked using his Atticus Finch voice. "I'd like a Jack Daniels on the rocks, please. What? Well, there must be some misunderstanding. I'm *Paul Timm.* Your boss, Buster Winston, is my good friend and I seriously doubt if he — Hello? Hello?"

Coming off a drunk is harsh but it only made Dad more crafty. He peeked at us and began a purposeful blubbering. "I really, really need a drink," he whined. "I can't stand this! I know I'll die if—"

The phone squawked. Dad plucked it expertly from the receiver. The hysterics instantly vanished. "Hello? This is Paul Timm." This time he imitated Sean Connery. "Oh, hi honey." It was Mom. His tremulous tone returned for her benefit. "Sweetheart, could you call Buster and ask if I can have a drink? What? Okay, I'll go to the ranch only if you meet me there. Quit your job. I'll give you money. Okay, here." He reluctantly gave me the phone.

He paced the room, mumbling.

Mom got a whispered earful from me about Dad's condition, the pit boss, and the mickey. That last thing made her quiet. I think I detected stifled laughter. The phone connection might have been faulty.

"Kristy, I forgot to tell you that Buster called a Reno doctor to come to the *Starlight* and give your father a shot. Something . . . *legal*—" She paused. I think she put her hand over the mouthpiece, "—that will relax him enough for you to get him on the plane. Good luck, sweetie."

Relief washed over me. We had an hour and a half until take-off.

During my conversation with Mom, Dad tried to get Phil to go downstairs for a bottle. Dad said he felt a spasm coming on as he clutched at his heart and started contracting his chest muscles to prove it. Phil took off his own shirt and showed Dad he could do it, too.

Twenty minutes passed and the physician arrived. Dad let him give the shot but after ten minutes, he showed no sign that the drug had been effective. Puzzled, the doctor gave him a second one. We had one hour left to catch that plane.

"Boy, it's rare to give two doses of this stuff," the doctor said, "but this should do it." Fifteen minutes later Dad was the same. Phil and I got nervous.

"This is unheard of," said the doctor, looking at us. "I'll follow you to the airport."

The bodyguards skillfully worked our little group through the casino and into the waiting hotel car, placing my father in the middle so he couldn't leap out the door.

Our flight took off in half an hour.

The five of us surrounded my wily father through the small lobby to the airliner door. There, the two hulking men told us they'd never met anyone like Dad. The doctor agreed, and covertly administered a third shot. Goodbyes and heartfelt thanks went around, and we were on our own.

Inside the aircraft, as Phil ushered a finally sleepy dad to our seats, I asked the flight attendant, in a low voice, to pass us by when drinks were served. I thought it best to leave out the part where if Dad saw the liquor he might get crazy and flail around like a lunatic. Her bouffant head nodded absently. Comforted, I sat down.

After fifteen minutes in the air, the drug finally kicked in and Dad napped between us. I felt at ease when the flight attendant's head bobbed into view. Her cart, covered with bar paraphernalia inched towards us, stopping by each passenger. Finally, she was a seat away. I smiled, confident she'd move on. Instead, she *paused* next to us. No recognition registered in her eyes. Phil and I stared at each other over Dad's snoring Germanic nose. Incredibly, she opened her mouth to speak. But an involuntary menacing expression on my face caused her to snap her mouth shut, straighten up, and move on. I guess I'd had enough.

Wade met our plane in Redmond. We were glad to be back in our simple ranching country. My father, subdued and malleable, got in the backseat of the Jeep and began snoring. Like the bodyguards, we flanked him, just in case. Two days later, he had recovered enough to stand with his lawyer and work out a deal with the county court, saving the ranch until the next crisis.

A week later, Buster wrote, "Thanks! FYI. In the future, a mickey will always be accessible for the girl with blonde braids."

He could have left that out.

ᘒᘒᘒ

Dad, the Vegas Girl, Mom, and the Slippery Slope

Winter of 1973: Phil and I were still in Portland getting ready to move to the ranch the next summer. Four boys, Wade, Rand, Ray, and Tom lived at the ranch to help Dad out while he flitted around the country. The boys were responsible for the ranch during this time and Mom helped out as much as she could while living in Bend, a good 130 miles away and a three-hour trip in good weather. Wade told us this story after the fact.

On a late winter afternoon at the ranch, the phone rang. Rand picked it up.

"Is tha' you, Rand?" Dad yelled through the old wall phone. "Mee' my plane in two hours a' the John Day airpor'. Make my bed up, I'm bringing someone." Click.

Rand didn't get a word in.

"Paul's coming?" asked Wade. "Well, he's flying in after dark then. The roads will be snowy on the way in, too." The phone squawked again.

"Hi Gam," Tom said, who had grabbed the receiver first. "Yeah, he just called. Said he's bringing someone. Probably Chuck or Bob to show them the ranch so he can get some money from 'em. Okay. I'll tell them. See you soon." Tom looked at the other three guys. "Gam's in Prineville, on her way. She's bringing doughnuts!"

Wade and Rand's friends, Tom and Ray, called Mom, Gam, too. When Wade was a baby, Gam was his version of Grandma and it stuck. Before he was a teenager, he called Dad, Tootie, but wouldn't be caught dead saying it at nineteen.

Rand spoke up. "Ray and I could go get him."

Wade looked at him. He knew that Rand, just seventeen, missed the city and liked to go into town more than the rest. Fearless, he had more accidents than the other boys, and the winter road conditions were dangerous. But Ray, also young, seemed wise beyond his years and a good companion to send with Rand.

"Okay, Rand," Wade told him, "go slow and straight to the airport. And, if he's drunk, or even if he's not, don't take him to the bar. No matter what he says. *Even if he bawls.* Remember, he's a good actor."

"Yeah, yeah. *Dad,*" Rand said. "We'll get home before midnight." Ray

36

and Rand got in Dad's Jeep Wagoneer and tore down the muddy ranch driveway towards town.

It wasn't long before Wade and Tom heard Mom's Toyota pulling into the ranch yard. Wade carried her suitcase into Dad's bedroom and left her to unpack, while the boys set out the doughnuts and made a fresh pot of coffee.

Tom glanced out the window and saw headlights. "Wade," he said. "Paul's here!"

Dad flung open the Wagoneer's door and toppled out, barely righting himself. "Who op'n ta door? I wasn' ready to ge' ou'," he said, looking around at the boys. A young gaunt woman dressed in purple hot pants and a skimpy lavender tank top peeked out.

"See, honey'? I tol' you I'm rich! I own everthi' you can see." He swept his arm in a semi-circle, barely missing smacking Tom, who ducked. Then remembering his rich, land-owner persona, Dad issued orders.

Tom noticed movement in the backseat and opened the Wagoneer's back door. A tiny little girl in pink polka dot shorts and a lightweight blouse emerged.

"Mommy, where are the horses?" the child asked, rubbing her sleepy eyes. "Uncle Paul said he had a brown one named Joe I could ride."

"Tom," slurred Dad, "bring blankees and pillow for Bobbie's lil' girl, Joanie, 'kay? She'll sleep on the couch. My bedroom's this way, Britt'y. "

"Paul, I'm Brenda and my little girl's name is Julie, 'member?" said the young woman, slightly tipsy herself. "Le' me pu' Julie down, firs', then I'll come."

"Arigh'," Dad agreed, turning too quickly and almost losing his footing a second time. The boys were trying not to watch the girl in the hot pants. "It's so col', here. Vegas was *sooo* warm when we too' offfff!"

Wade started to speak up. "Paul—"

"Brinadrinkay?" Dad asked, as he fumbled his way to the back bedroom, bouncing side to side off the walls and finally landing on the king-size bed.

"Two drin's. An' leave the botl'. An' show Barbie where ah 'm in case she go' loss. She'll sleee here wi' me."

Rand volunteered to fetch the young woman while Ray brought the drinks.

Everyone crowded into Dad's bedroom.

"C'mere honey," said Dad. "Here's m' be'. Yer stay here wi' me."

37

"Well, Mr. Timm," said Mom, sitting unnoticed on a chair behind the open door. "Where will I sleep, then?"

As if poked by an electric cattle prod, the sound of Mom's voice jolted Dad so badly that he fell off the other side of the bed. But within seconds, he sprang up like a jack-in-the-box and looked frantically around.

"Di' you boys hear tha'?" Dad whispered, plucking nervously at his shirt front and scrubbing his head, making his hair stand on end. "Oh, God! Maybe I've ha' too mush booze. Is finally happen'. I've gone off the deep en' an' instea' of pink elephn's I hear Dar's voice!"

"Patootie," Mom said. "I'm real all right."

"Oooooh, Dar'!" spotting her in the chair behind the door. "Honey! You know I love you bes'!" Dad pleaded. "Of course you'll slee' wi' me. Why, Beulah can happ'ly slee' wi' the boys. Righ' boys?"

The boys muttered, heartily agreeing with Dad.

"Yes, it's only good manners—" said Tom.

"My bed's biggest—" said Rand.

"I'm oldest, dammit—!" said Wade.

"Well, I helped pick her up at the airport, brought her overnight bag in—" offered Ray.

"Boys!" Mom admonished. "Brenda's a guest and she will sleep with her little girl on the biggest bed upstairs. Your bed, Rand. You'll sleep on the couch tonight."

The young woman sat on the end of the bed. Mom put her arm around Brenda and led her out to Julie.

"I'll jus' wai' here, Dar', honey!" said Dad, who was also sitting on the bed. "Don' worry. Belinda's's jush a fren'. I luff oly you."

Dejected, the boys trailed out.

The morning came slow in the steep little valley—the sun hesitant to rise. Coffee perked on the stove when Dad showed up in his bright kitchen. His hair was so mussed it looked like a porcupine crouched on his head. The little girl concentrated on Mom's buttermilk pancakes with warm syrup and melting bits of butter.

"Linda," Dad said. "I'm sending you back to Vegas today. I've arranged the flight. Here's five hundred dollars. Sorry 'bout all this. Dart's my ex-wife but I still love her."

"It's *Brenda* and it's okay, Paul," the woman said. "At least Julie and I got to take a mini vacation and see a ranch."

At that moment, a loud thumping and cursing came from above and on the stairs. At the bottom of the stairs, a large mound of bodies made up of the boys.

"Git off my head—!"

"Ray! That's my hand you're grinding into the floor—"

"Move off of my back or I swear—"

"Oooh! You'll what? I'm so scared!"

"Boys!" said Mom. "We have company, remember?"

A chorus of mumbled hellos came from the pile.

"One of you has to take Brenda and her daughter to the airport," said Dad. "I'd take them but I want to show Dart something up Schoolhouse Gulch."

"Remember," Mom told Brenda. "Be brave and watch after your daughter. She needs you."

"Thanks, Mrs. Timm," Brenda said, dabbing her pretty brown eyes. "I feel I've known you all my life."

After Brenda departed, this time with Wade and Tom, Dad took Mom up the draw behind the old schoolhouse. Supposedly to show her a newly developed spring. On the way up, the truck angled sideways on the dirt road, but they made it to the top.

"Dart, can we get back together? I'm sorry about the girl."

"I think we enjoy each other best this way, Paul."

"Dammit. Okay. Well, guess we better head back." He turned the truck around and headed down the draw but, unexpectedly, the truck lost traction in the thick mud and slid sideways, closer and closer into a steep gully.

"AAAAAAHHH," they yelled together. Dad yanked the steering wheel; the truck righted, but landed in the middle of the gully and the mud was so slick the truck began to slide, picking up speed. Both sets of wheels were perfectly aligned on each side, pointing downhill, with the deep gully a V under the carriage.

"DO SOMETHING, PAUL!"

"WE'LL HAVE TO RIDE IT OUT!" Dad yelled. "THERE'S NO WAY TO GET OUT EXCEPT AT THE BOTTOM!"

The truck rocketed wildly down toward the highway, pitching into boulders and small junipers. Mom pushed her hands against the ceiling to keep from bouncing up and hitting her head.

"AAAHH!"

"AAAAHHH!"

Finally, the truck lurched forward and right out of the gully, before it hit the highway fence and stopped. Mom and Dad sat quietly in disbelief of their good fortune. After a few minutes, Mom smiled and looked at Dad.

"Just like our marriage was. Adventurous but a slippery slope. We're lucky we came out of it alive!"

ᏊᏊᏊ

Dad and His Hired Men

"Honey, I've hired a guy," said Dad, over the phone. "Has a wife and twin babies. Staying in the ranch house. His name is Colton Marsdale. Coming today. Love you." Click.

"Great news, Phil," I said, sliding his eggs and bacon onto the plate. "Now we can concentrate on our leather work." We didn't pretend to know ranch stuff, but we helped out a few hours a day. It was right to help because Dad let us live on the ranch. The only problem was, unless we sold our leatherwork, we had no money coming in. Dad needed an all-around hand.

"Nice to meet you," I said as we all shook hands. "You're a godsend." Colton appeared eager. His wife beamed. The babies gurgled. All was well.

"We're here to work," the man said. "I grew up on a ranch, and I can ride anything. Jody can cook for your dad. You can trust us, too."

Wow. They sounded great. Maybe a little cocky and boastful, but young people did that sometimes. Colton also told us he had a cousin, Larry (a skinny Frankenstein), who irrigated. Dad hired him, too. Larry lived in the bunkhouse. After Dad made some surprise visits and the Marsdales got used to it, he and they got along fine.

It seemed too good to be true. So time passed, yet an unexplained niggling began in my brain. But being a pessimist, I gave my brain a good hard wallop on its backside—if my brain had a backside. I decided to practice the gift-horse mouth philosophy.

A few months later, the Marsdales showed up at our door declaring that they needed to go to town or back to Prineville to do family stuff. We let it pass, but it got to be habitual—a couple times a week, with overnights increasing to two or three nights away from the ranch.

On occasion, Phil would go up to Dad's house in early afternoon to get something from the barn. One afternoon, Colton came out of the house yawny and sleepy-eyed.

41

"Hi Phil," he said. "Just taking the day off. I'm caught up on work. Nothin' to do right now."

Phil looked around the driveway. The corrals had broken boards, old barbed wire lay in twisted and intertwined piles, the barn door hung off its hinge, and lots of other immediate, obvious chores remained undone.

Colton, who already decided Phil didn't know as much as he did, saw this. "Hell, I wasn't hired to do *those* chores," he said. "I only cowboy and do the hay work!"

"Did you tell Paul this?" Phil asked. "He should know."

"Yes, I did," he said. "I told him. He was fine with it."

Phil didn't have enough information to challenge the guy, so he kept his own counsel until he had time to talk to Dad.

Another month went by, and a call came from Portland. Phil's aunt and uncle were celebrating their golden wedding anniversary. We needed to go but couldn't take our young dog, Rooster, so we asked the Marsdales if they could keep him for two days. Colton really liked Rooster.

"Sure!" he said. "We'll keep the little guy for ya. He can follow my tractor with my dog while I poison rats on the meadow."

"No!" Phil said. "My dog wouldn't eat the poisoned grain when sprinkled on the ground, but he would eat the sage rats that eat the poisoned grain. He's half Siberian Husky and there isn't much he wouldn't eat."

"That's not a problem. My dog eats them all the time and he's alive," said Colton, not meeting Phil's eyes. "But I'll leave Rooster home."

Two days later we stood at the door of Dad's ranch house.

"Hell, I don't know where Rooster is," said Colton. "He took off." The Marsdales were packing to *leave* the ranch. They couldn't have appeared more guilty.

Frantic, we stopped at every ranch house in Izee asking if they'd seen Rooster. No one had. A sickening feeling crept over us. We headed back to the ranch for another conversation with Colton Marsdale. No sign of him, his wife and their babies, but Larry was standing in the driveway.

"Still no luck?" he said. "You know, I remember when Colton poisoned the rats in the field, Rooster was with him. That's the last time I saw the pup."

"Colton took Rooster with him when he poisoned?" Phil asked, incredulous. Larry was so forthcoming, it was obvious Colton hadn't told him that we'd asked him to keep Rooster at home.

"Yes," said Larry. "And that night I heard an animal crying."

42

Phil found our Rooster, dead, under the front doorstep of Dad's ranch-house a couple of months after Colton had let him eat his fill of poisoned rats.

***

"Skinny Frankenstein" stayed on. At first all was well. Wade returned from Vegas and helped Larry. The four of us branded Dad's cattle, and moved cattle to the pasture on Dad's forest permits. All seemed uneventful and quiet. Turns out it was that calm-before-the-storm thing.

"Larry has women's underwear in his drawers," Wade told us. "I was putting away his cleaned laundry and saw them."

"Well," I said. "If the man wants to wear women's undies under his drawers, who am I to judge?"

"No, in his *bureau* drawers. And Paul makes Larry wait on him, bring him drinks. He even has to sleep at the foot of his bed. Larry's been getting drunk, too."

"Another alcoholic?" I said. "How did we miss it?"

Each time Dad left, Larry took off to town to drink in bars. He brought back scruffy alcoholics to stay on the ranch, let them charge food at Chester's grocery store, and paid for drinks at the bar on Dad's tab. He stayed longer in town than he worked at the ranch. The three of us unanimously agreed to fire Larry. We headed to town.

Phil and Wade walked into the dark bar on Main Street. Phil went up to Larry, who was surrounded by his drinking cronies.

"I'm sorry but you're fired," Phil told him. "No reason to come back to Izee. I've brought all your gear." Larry's bar friends made some drunken murmurings.

"Oh . . . well, uh, did you remember the women's underwear?" asked Larry. "It's taken me years to collect those."

***

Dad spent time in all the taverns in Grant County and beyond. Each held prospective hired men for him to pick from. Walter Joe, a Native American, hung out in Paulina. That was good enough for Dad, so he hired him. Elvin, the proprietor of the tavern, told Dad that Walter Joe was a recovering alcoholic. Maybe they weren't a good match, he said to Dad.

"Nah," slurred Dad. "I'm not an alcoholic, so it's okay."

Elvin just stared at Dad. Walter Joe worked hard for a while, but three weeks later at 4 a.m., someone banged on our door.

"Who?" snorfled Phil. "Who?"

BAMBAMBAAMBAM.

43

"Phil," I whispered. "You're making owl noises, and someone's pounding on the door. The Hell's Angels are back for real this time."

Phil got up and crept to the door. I grabbed the shotgun next to the bed. Phil unlocked the door and eased it open an inch. They both talked fast. Then the door shut.

"Walter Joe. He's drunk," said Phil. "Told me your dad wants him to take old batteries to town and sell them. He's in Paul's old pickup. I told him to go back to the ranch and I'd follow. He also said Paul shot at him. Got to make sure Paul's okay."

"What? Shouldn't we call the sheriff? You might get shot. Do we have any armor around?"

Phil left. He called from Dad's within a half hour. "Walter Joe isn't here. Paul's passed out," said Phil. "The place is trashed and it looks like they fought. Walter Joe took the guns. One is your grandfather's shotgun. I've called Elvin at Paulina to alert them."

That evening Elvin called us back. "Walter Joe went straight to the bar," he explained. "I nabbed the keys and rifles, and the sheriff nabbed Walter Joe. His story is he and Paul got drunk. Walter Joe bogarted the Jack Daniels. They scuffled around the living room. Paul threatened Walter Joe with an unloaded shotgun and crouched behind the sofa. Walter Joe had the other unloaded gun and hunkered behind a chair. They yelled 'I'm-gonna-get-you' back and forth until Paul passed out. Walter Joe loaded the batteries and guns and high-tailed out of there. He stopped at your house to throw off suspicion and give himself time. It played out like a good western. But in this one, the line is fuzzy between the good and the bad guys!"

❧❧❧

Pop

"Here, Pop" Phil said. "Take this shovel to help move the cattle in the corral. We're trying to separate the calves from the mothers and the bulls."

"Where do I stand, son?"

"Away from that gate, see it over there? That's where they go in."

"Oh. Okay."

A half hour later, Pop was standing in the middle of the herd, waving his hands at the cattle we were trying to move to the gate behind him. The animals stopped dead in their tracks.

"Dad! You need to move out of the way!"

"Okay. Closer and more hand waving, right?" With renewed vigor, he shouted and waved, and pushed the cows toward the gate they had just come through. Wade sprinted to the gate just before they poured out back onto the meadow. Pop decided to yell and scream at the herd as they tried to get closer to the opening where Phil wanted them to go. Pop's eyes took on a feverish look, and he swung the shovel like a horizontal pendulum, cutting a wide swath as the cattle bellowed and backed up from the dervish in front of them.

"POP! Please, please move! Not that way!"

"You want them to go away? Alright . . . I got it! Don't worry!" He moved (with what seemed to be the speed of light) into the herd, screaming and jumping with his shovel, waving it like a semaphore high above the cows' heads.

Phil and Wade rushed to the edges, keeping the animals bunched, but in the middle was a wild man. The group wheeled and hoofed it around the flailing creature and into the corral they were supposed to enter—except for one bull that rushed Pop. The guys couldn't react fast enough to get Pop out of its way. They watched the scene with horror. The snorting black Angus rushed at Pop, who lifted his shovel and bonked it hard on the head. The bull pivoted, circled, and re-joined the herd.

"It's a helluva good thing I helped you guys today," said Pop, with a happy smile on his face. "With all your extra shenanigans and running around disturbing the cows, you would've never got these animals done."

***

"Not sure how I feel about leaving the ranch for a couple of days," Phil said, "with Pop there." We watched the wipers move the snow off the Jeep Wagoneer's window. The snow was sticking on the road as we drove over Mt. Hood.

"Although, what could happen?" Phil added. "Mom's there, too. I'm sure it'll be fine. Elk season's over. I have an elk hanging in the shed."

Meanwhile, at the beach, three hundred miles away, on the other side of the Cascades, we were enjoying a brief time off from the ranch. After dinner the phone rang.

"When are you coming back?" Pop said. "I'm worried about the elk going bad."

"I only shot it a couple of days ago, Dad," said Phil. "It's fine."

"I'm thinking about cutting it up."

"What? Why? No! It's okay. It can hang for a couple of weeks yet."

"I don't think it can. I'm worried."

"It's fine, Dad."

"Okay, but maybe you should come back."

"I'll be back in two days. Bye, Dad."

The wind brought an autumn storm to the beach, and we enjoyed it from inside. The rain pushed against the windows, and the ocean swells rose high on the deserted shoreline.

Riiiing!!

"I decided it would keep better if I cut it in half." Sweat appeared on Phil's brow. "So I used the electric chain saw and ripped it right down the back bone." Visions of the mess that the chain saw had made—scattering bone chips, bits of elk hair, coagulated blood, and other elk gook all over the rest of the carcass—were running through Phil's mind. Not to mention the extra work that would be needed to clean all that up when we took it to the meat cutter.

"No need to thank me son."

***

On another occasion before leaving the ranch for a brief holiday, Phil left directions with Pop concerning the weed spraying and also with the pilot who would be doing the aerial spraying.

"The weed spraying is all set up with the crop duster for spraying the Whitetop in the meadows and on the hills," said Phil. "The pilot promised to stay away from the river. He has good instructions."

Phil's interest in the ranch's welfare grew roots, so to speak. He'd set up a yearly program to get rid of a noxious weed called Whitetop that the cattle, deer, and elk wouldn't eat. It had been spreading into the crop land since 1977. Good advice from the Soil Conservation Service helped Phil to begin a restorative plan for the ranch. That plan included weed control, as well as the planting of willows and other shrubs that would help to stabilize the stream banks and cool the river, ultimately helping the fish. This was accomplished with the volunteer help of friends, family, and agencies.

Phil had become a steward of the land. Pop and Dad didn't understand the importance of it but didn't discourage Phil from doing it either; they just couldn't see the changes needed to restore the ranch, or the long-term benefits to the fish and to our cattle.

Anyhow, the trip relaxed us. It was nice to take a break. And after five worry-free days away, we headed home early, arriving when the sun was still barely peeking over the desert mountains.

The sprayed areas were already brown. Unfortunately *everything* was brown and dying; including the willows along the river.

"Oh, no!" Phil said. "Why did the guy spray the river corridor? It's all dead. All the plantings!"

Phil called his folks. Mom answered.

"Mom," said Phil. "The pilot made a huge mistake! I told him, specifically, to leave the river alone! All that effort, by so many people — gone. Dead."

"Well, honey," said Mom. "It wasn't just the pilot. When the pilot arrived, your father gave him last-minute instructions. I heard him tell the pilot to spray everywhere—up and down the river, too. Your dad won't admit it, but he feels terrible. It won't help things to get mad at him."

So, to keep the peace, Phil didn't, as is the case in many father-son relationships. Usually, they could laugh it off or dismiss the problem, but not this time.

***

But, on another occasion, they could. As the herd ambled down the road with the dogs ranging back and forth behind them, everything was peaceful. Phil and I rode quietly as we headed to our forest permit. It was one of those rare cattle drives where nothing was going wrong. The cows, dogs and horses, all smiled. Even the horseflies smiled. Mom and Pop were due back from town. In fact, we heard the Toyota coming up behind us.

"Where do you want us, son?" Pop asked, grinning, as he rolled his window down. "In front?"

"No Dad. I think we can handle it."

"Don't be afraid to ask, Phil. We'll help. After all, they're our cows, so we should help." With that he gunned the engine and drove a foot behind the straggling calves. Honking.

The herd galvanized and split down the middle. A few hurdled over the fences on each side of the highway. Some, upset about their calves, bumped the Toyota. Mammas mooed, looking for their babies who had shot off in terror when the honking started.

HONK! HONK! Pop kept his hand on the horn.

"STOP DAD!! STOP HONKING." But Pop couldn't hear over his horn. "DAAAAAAD! STOP!!!"

We couldn't do a thing. The cattle wanted to get away from the boogeyman and scattered everywhere. Some headed towards home. Phil and I rode feverishly trying to gather and bunch the herd. The dogs followed the strays down the steep banks. Some cows jumped the barbed wire into the neighbor's meadow. Phil rode hard to catch up to the Toyota.

"You can go on home, Dad!" Phil yelled over the cacophony.

"That's okay, son. We'll go to the entrance to the forest service and wait on the road to turn them in."

"NO!" Phil yelled at Pop's retreating rig. "Please go home!!" Pop waved out the truck window.

For forty-five minutes, we worked hard to get the cows back together before heading up the highway with them. Man and beast panted and sweated with the effort. After another half hour, we all calmed down and moved gently along the asphalt. A mile away from our turn-in spot, Phil dashed ahead, keeping to the side of the herd until he reached the truck. It was parked a couple of yards from the entrance; the cows wouldn't have gone in with it so close.

Phil leaned down toward Pop's open window. I watched as Phil's arms flung out to the heavens, then down at his sides, then a pleading stance. He resembled a conductor directing *The Ride of the Valkyries*. Soon he trotted back.

"I convinced him to move farther away from the entrance," Phil said, his voice barely there. "I told him that the spot was a dangerous one for log trucks coming up on him, but if he went up another quarter mile, he'd be safe."

As we watched, Pop maneuvered the Toyota directly across from the forest road, maybe ten yards away from its original spot. Getting the cows past him would be nigh impossible.

Exasperated, we looked at each other. "Oh, what the heck," Phil said. "Pop loves this. We'll handle the cows somehow."

And we did.

☙☙☙☙

Pop (Again)

In spite of having Crohn's Disease, slow-growing prostate cancer, and rheumatoid arthritis, Phil's dad, Pop, was a force to be reckoned with. He had a unique way of dealing with illness or misfortune. A friendly man to strangers, he confided in them—sort of brought them into his realm of existence. Whether they wanted it or not. Usually, it happened when we were with him. It was a wild ride every time.

The usual symptoms showed up as red flags for Pop's prostate, so we got to go on lots of trips to Bend together to his urologist appointments. Moments to be cherished, in hindsight. And speaking of hindsight. . .

Gobs of breakfast food materialized before us as if Glenda, the good witch in *Wizard of Oz*, just waved her wand and it appeared. One of the perks of Pop's trips was we had wondrous meals on the road.

"I dearly love biscuits an' gravy, honey," Pop told our waitress. "Had it when I was a boy in Tennessee. Mama made it from our freshly butchered pig. My brothers always got the backstrap, even though I fed and watered and cleaned up after that pig. Had to carry the feed and water a mile."

"Well now," said the waitress. "That's just awful. You'd think your mother would stick up for you, huh?"

"Oh, my mama worked awful hard running a boarding house, you know," Pop told her. "My daddy was gassed in World War I and too sick to help. He died early. Us eight kids had to figure out things ourselves."

The waitress liked Pop and had to tear herself away to go work. We'd heard the stories already so we tucked in and ate, not fully understanding the treasure of Pop and his life stories. The hurt of the unfairness he faced because of his brothers and sisters was clear in his voice, but he needed to tell it. It was like the telling helped him deal with it. The waitress returned to top off our coffee.

"Where y'all headed?" she asked. "Bend or over the Cascades to the valley?"

"Bend," said Pop. "To the *doctor*. But if that bastard tries to go up my ass again, I'll—"

"—Uh," said Phil. "Could we have the check please?"

"—kill him!" said Pop. "He does it every time! He must enjoy—"

"—Could you tell me where the restroom is?" I asked. "And could we have the boxes for the extra food?" A giggle threatened to erupt. Giggling might hurt Pop's feelings but, boy, it was hard. A rundown of the alphabet in my head helped.

"—old men's asses."

"Uh huh," said the waitress. "Well, got to get back to my other tables." A quick glance at Phil, and Mom revealed an all-consuming interest in a dying bush outside the window or the fascinating parking lot. A grease spot on the table required my attention. Pop was in a particularly good mood. He loved to visit with people no matter what the subject matter.

***

Pop wanted to help with ranch work. It didn't matter that he was in his late seventies or that his health was tenuous. Building a new fence was quick gratification. Phil was constructing a pasture fence that ran north and south behind the Poison Creek ranch house. Pop was crippled from his "arthuritis" so he rode the fence line on his three-wheeler. Three wheelers are dangerous on flat ground let alone hills—even gradual hills. Pop was nearest to me when he raced by, hit a three-inch rock, and lurched over sideways. The engine raced as it tipped over, and Pop dove off in a tuck-and-roll down the slope. A professional stunt man couldn't have done any better.

"Great dive, Pop! I give it a ten!" I yelled. "Are you okay?"

"Yeah, hit a damn rock," he said. "Going too fast."

"You're getting back on?" I asked. "Why not take a good nap and/or a shot of Wild Turkey?"

"No. Gotta help Phil get this damn fence done. I could die tomorrow, then what kind of help would I be?"

***

Pop and Mom were always working and helping on various projects on their ranch, and not *only* on the ranch. When I decided to go back to school, I asked Pop and Mom if they could help me video my eight-minute run for a college physical health class. The class required the completion of an audio and video of a series of exercises, including running an eight-minute mile. Phil had ranch jobs to finish, so Pop and Mom kindly said yes. Pop would film me from the back of the Toyota pickup, and Mom would drive. The camera was an early model camcorder, difficult to hold on his shoulder for any length of time.

The run started at our house and ended a little past the Poison Creek gate. Phil's watch was strapped on my wrist.

"This isn't going to be easy," I said, "because I don't usually run this fast. I have to do it right the first time." Mom and Pop nodded. We got in our positions.

"Here we go!" I said.

Mom eased the Toyota onto the road, and Pop sat on a lawn chair in back and started filming. The stick-shift caused an unsteady acceleration.

"Jane!" yelled Pop. "Don't jerk so much, it's hard to film!"

I'd waited until they were slightly ahead before running but, before long, I almost passed them. "You can go faster, Mom."

Mom couldn't hear me inside the rig, so I waved my hand in a forward motion. She gently accelerated but Pop toppled forward off his perch.

"Jane! Slow down! Tell me before you go faster!"

"Did you say faster?" Mom said. "Okay!" Pop fell off the chair again, and the camera filmed a close-up of his right boot.

"JANE! Good God Almighty!" yelled Pop. "I said *slow* down! I'm getting a damn leg cramp!"

Mom took her foot off the gas, causing Pop to topple backwards, filming the sky. His lips moved, and I assumed he was grumbling curse words.

I waved at Mom to speed up. We were halfway and I could hardly breathe. The sound of a rig broke into my thoughts. *Great. Neighbors are going to witness my death. Or, worse, Pop's.* I waved and flashed a big smile and upped the pace as they drove past. As soon as they were out of sight, I slowed and sucked in gulping breaths. I looked up at Pop and saw he was filming the neighbor's dog in the back of the rig.

Pop was settling in and filming, but I was catching up to them so I waved at Mom again.

Mom slowly stepped on the gas, almost sending Pop flying off towards the side. He dropped the camera in the pickup bed as he grabbed the side of the truck

"JANE! ARE YOU TRYING TO KILL ME?"

"Stop yelling at me, Jack! That's unnecessary. I'm trying to be careful."

"Kristy, I don't think I can hold it up and film any longer. I'm about dead."

"Pop, look!" I wheezed at him, knocking at death's door myself. "See that apple tree on the left side of the road? That's where we stop."

"Okay, I'll try. It's damned heavy," he said, gasping and panting. "Hope I make it."

We did, and later that evening . . .

"Ohhhh! Hahahahahahaha." Mom, Phil and I choked with laughter two minutes into the film; tears running down our faces, cheeks sore, chests heaving. Seated on the floor, I rolled over onto my stomach, pounding the floor with unbridled glee.

Pop stared at the screen, a tiny frown on his face. "I don't see what's so damn funny. I really hurt! You have no idea—"

That set us off again—laughing harder than before, and each new scene better than the previous one. Pretty soon we heard . . .

"Heh, heh, heh," said Pop. "Hahahaha. That is funny, come to think of it. Hahahahaha! I should be an actor!" Finally, that Tennessee humor broke through and when he got it, his sense of humor was one of the best out there.

Later, two or three weeks after submitting the video to the physical health professor and not hearing from him, I called.

"Did you say Kristy St. Clair?" asked the professor. "Oh yes. It made the rounds. Great entertainment! You got an A! Was that your father-in-law? What a funny fellow!"

Yeah. He was irascible but a fun guy, too.

Thanks, Pop.

 ᏣᏣᏣ

FAMILY

Family makes up the core of ranch life, and my nephew Wade became involved as a young man. Here is his story...

Wade

Just seventeen when Wade arrived at the ranch in 1972, he immediately got involved in ranch activities. He'd spent a snowy winter up Poison Creek at the main ranch house; mostly alone. Dad was gone ninety percent of the time. Neighbors couldn't help liking Wade, while at the same time they were curious about the boy with the long black hair and skinny frame. They may have been leery at first, but not after Wade stopped at their houses, introduced himself, and asked for advice on ranch stuff. Something about Wade made him appealing and vulnerable.

Over the years, even after Dad died and Phil's folks bought the ranch, Wade visited often, helping us out or joining us during hunting season. He was always a part of the ranch. Wade also helped out other Izee families with branding, moving herds, and doing various ranch chores while learning from them at the same time. The Sheehans were one of those families.

Angus Sheehan stood next to his corral fence preparing a rope. His loop ready, he climbed onto his horse in the corral. Wade stood nearby while John organized the disinfectant and sharpened Angus's knife. They were getting ready to geld the young stallion that was pacing around the pen. John gave Wade a quick rundown of the scenario and what job he needed to be ready to do.

"Wade!" Angus bellowed. "We have to ketch 'n tie 'em up first. Just watch and wait 'til I tell you we're ready." In a flash he snatched his rope and threw the loop high around the horse's neck. The young horse turned to Angus and fought the loop, pulling back and cutting his air off. Soon, the horse went down and lay on its side.

"Go, Wade," Angus hollered. "Get on his head before he hurts himself flailing around!"

John, Wade and Gwen, John's wife, ran over to calm the frightened animal. As soon as the horse quieted, John started a complicated system of loops and half-hitches with a soft, heavy cotton rope that wound from the neck and front legs to the back legs and butt, and resembled a figure eight.

54

This was meant to gently control the horse on the ground and also to protect the men working on him. Wade's careful observance would help him to learn and remember.

"The only thing we can't tie is the head," explained John. "So, if you could continue to sit on it and hold its head down, that would be great. Shouldn't be a problem. Dad says the horse is too small to cause a ruckus."

Wade squatted down, settling his hands and knees on the horse's neck and head.

Angus brought his disinfected knife over. He knelt and grabbed the scrotum. The horse jerked hard. Wade wasn't totally prepared, and, with all the Sheehans watching, he sailed through the air and landed on his back. Within moments, he was on his feet again, scrambling to hold the head once more. Angus quickly made a slit in the sack and exposed the testicles. He separated the sperm ducts from the blood vessel cord. Angus used a clamp-like tool called the Emasculator to pinch off the blood cord, and then cut the sperm ducts.

"Sorry, Wade!" Angus shouted and chuckled at the same time. "Oh my, *heh, heh*. Oh gosh. *Heh, heh*, the look on your face . . . guess I startled 'im when I grabbed his scrotum. But I thought, he's a small horse. . . *heh, heh* . . . it won't be nothing to worry about. *Heh, heh, heh*. Guess I was wrong. Good job, Wade. Thanks for your help."

***

On another morning in summer, Wade maneuvered the old Chevy pickup over the rutty dry road as he headed north up Rosebud. Two miles up, a horse and rider stood next to the barbed-wire gate of the Timm/Sloan border fence. The horseman was Shane Gallagher.

"Hey, Wade!" yelled Shane. "You came along at the right time. I noticed a fat yearling steer sporting Paul's brand with porky quills all over his nose!"

"How do we get them out?" Wade asked. "We don't have a chute and head catch."

"We'll do it the old-fashioned way," Shane said as he readied his rope. "Now open that gate for me?"

Wade opened the gate, allowing Shane and his horse through. Wade then closed the gate and walked over to Shane and the horse.

"Here's what we'll do. I'll rope the steer. You run in and pluck the quills out." With that, Shane swung his rope over his head and tossed it onto the head of the steer. He backed up his horse and tried to keep the rope taut while the steer backed against it. Wade loped over, bent down, and pulled out some quills with his bare hands.

BAAAHHH! BAAAAHHHH! The steer charged forward and chased Wade. "Jeez! Sorry Shane. Didn't expect him to be so upset! I'll get them next time."

"No, boy. I'm to blame. I shoulda been aware. Let's try it again, okay?"

Wade nodded and crept closer to the steer. As Shane pulled tight again, Wade rushed the steer and yanked out a few more quills. The steer got extra snorty and pulled against the rope, looking for his assailant. Wade had already hoofed it back to the fence.

"Doing good, son," Shane said. "Let's try 'er again." Shane's voice sounded odd. He had pulled his kerchief up over his mouth. *Probably because of the dust,* Wade thought. *Almost sounded like the man was coughing, too.* Well, anyway, Wade had a plan.

"Here goes," yelled Shane in a muffled voice. "This one'll do it!"

In a second, Wade was on top of it. He worked madly around the muzzle while the steer bumped and rolled and humped up, trying to free itself from the monster on its back.

"UUUHHH! MMMAAAA!" the steer screamed while it heaved and twisted. Wade rolled off, but it seemed that Shane was letting the rope slip, allowing the steer to come for Wade like a locomotive running hot on coal. Shane tightened the rope again, choking the steer down.

"Now go in there," he said, "and pull the loop off its head as soon as I give it slack. Don't worry. He won't have any fight left in him now."

Even so, Wade darted away as soon as the steer was loose. Wade looked over and noticed that Shane was bent over the saddle. *Hope he isn't having a heart attack. Is it normal for someone's shoulders to shake like that during a heart attack?*

"Well, we got it done, Wade. Good work," Shane said in a wavering voice. "I'll head back."

Wade watched as Shane rolled up his rope and trotted away. Strangely, after he closed the gate, Wade thought he heard laughing that lasted quite a while—even after he'd finished fixing the fence. *Boy, the coyotes are sure yapping.*

***

A few years later, after Dad died and Phil's folks bought the ranch, Wade was visiting during elk season. He'd gone far up Poison Creek draw in the afternoon to hunt.

Further down the draw and inside the ranch house, Mom and Pop were relaxing in overstuffed chairs, reading their books, while the living room fireplace glowed and the smell of smoldering juniper permeated the air.

56

Outside, the fall wind turned the leaves into gliders, and bare branches of the Silver Maple scraped the window. Confetti snow fell. The thermometer had dropped 15 degrees by the time darkness covered Poison Creek. Suddenly Mom and Pop heard pounding on the door.

"Who's there?" Pop yelled. "Show yourself!"

Wade's smiling face peeked through the snowy hood of his down jacket.

"I got an elk, Jack," said Wade. "But I need help getting it on the pulley."

"You're a damned liar, son," Pop said. "You didn't get an elk by yourself."

"Come look."

Mom and Pop followed Wade outside and sure enough, he'd killed his first cow elk. Out since midday, he'd finally tracked one down. Inside the shop, Pop hooked up a pulley, and they lifted the carcass.

"He'll hang for a couple of days," Pop said. "C'mon in the house and warm up. I'll buy you a drink."

Wade followed, scuffing snow and dirt as he walked the driveway to the house. Adrenaline still coursed through his body, but he could feel the weight of fatigue coming on.

When they got inside, Mom poured a couple of shots of Wild Turkey for the men, and they settled near the fire.

"Okay," said Pop. "Tell us how it went."

"I hunted close to the old Poison Creek road hoping something would pass by," Wade told them. "Sure enough, two cows and their calves came down the draw I hunkered in. Got a shot off and dropped a cow."

"Oh hell," said Pop. "You're still a damned liar."

Wade grinned. "She died instantly. I worried another hunter might stroll down from the forest and claim it if I went for help to load it, so I wrangled it up into the back of the Toyota—"

"Son, it's at least 500 to 600 pounds, and you loaded it yourself into the back of that tiny car?"

"Jack," said Wade, "you don't see anyone else with me do you? Must be 'cause I was so excited, it being my first elk and all."

Pop gave him a cockeyed look. "Well, son," said Pop. "Here's to youth!"

OCCASIONS

When we recall the past we usually find it is the simplest things—not the great occasions—that in retrospect give off the greatest glow of happiness.

~Bob Hope

Paulina Rodeo

The summer day would be a scorcher as we traveled west forty-two miles to the tiny settlement of Paulina to attend their annual rodeo. Visiting us for the weekend were Phil's folks, my sister Paige, and her two little girls, Tori and Carli. Dad also flew in for the weekend and promised to show up. Paulina's rodeo is an amateur event with ranchers from miles around attending, including my neighbors. My brother competed in professional rodeos for years as a bronc and bull rider, so I was excited to see what the day would bring.

In the middle of Paulina sat a one-story building that housed a grocery store and gas station, a tavern, and a post office. Other evidences of a township were a church, a school, and a community hall. The rodeo was a mile west. We turned into a wide, dirt parking area that resembled a wrecking yard of old full-sized sedans, pickups, motor homes, and travel trailers, all jammed together. John Sheehan, an Izee neighbor, had just pulled in too, so we parked near him.

"Since this is your first visit to the rodeo," he said as we all strolled together toward the rodeo grounds, "you oughta know that you might see a fight. Some young bucks or even a rancher or two are likely to get liquored up."

I glanced at Phil's parents, and his mom had a dubious expression on her attractive face, but Phil's father had perked up. He'd boxed in his youth and was still muscular at sixty-three. My sister and I exchanged a look. We knew about fighting. Our brother, although built small, had *loved* rodeo brawls.

In spite of the odds of seeing fisticuffs, our family group continued to the rodeo site. Topping a hill, we saw the bleachers already filled, so people now sprawled on packed dirt paths that had been terraced and designed as a small amphitheater. Spectators had blankets or pads to sit on, but we had only our rear ends. Pop's face fell as he looked down at our only option.

"Rahtcheer?" Phil's dad said, incredulous. "My authuritis will kill me if I sit heer!" His Tennessee roots revealed themselves when he got excited.

"Come on, Jack," Phil's mom told him. "Let's just sit down and watch."

"I just know sittin' heer's gonna be hell," he said, loud enough to wake up God. "My hemorrhoids just can't take it!" Folks within a three-mile radius were now aware of the greenhorns' arrival— particularly the one with hemorrhoids.

A loudspeaker near the arena screeched out the name and competition number of the next bronc rider. Pop's attention thankfully shifted to the unfortunate young rider getting a stomping by his bucking horse down in the arena. With the rodeo starting, we plopped down in the dirt, managing different sitting postures—even Pop, although he kept up a running conversation about his condition.

An uncomfortable and sweltering hour passed as the corral goings-on switched from broncs to bull riding. The contestants were modern-day gladiators getting beat to pieces. Ninety-nine percent of them sprung up from the dirt flashing a happy smile after a horse or bull's hoof scraped off layers of skin from their faces or hands. They'd jump up and stagger off to their waiting friends who, not five minutes before, were laughing and egging them on. A couple of unfortunates lay still until an ambulance arrived and hauled them to a hospital in Prineville, an hour away.

My young nieces didn't give a hoot about the rodeo but *did* notice the smell of burgers cooking in a shack next to the arena. Reluctantly, my sister herded them down to the food booth. They were prim eaters, so when clouds of powdery dust from the rodeo activities enveloped the food source, I knew they'd return burgerless. I also spotted John Sheehan coming back toward us, hauling a couple of quart-sized buckets of beer and a few paper cups. His dad, Angus, wasn't with him. Angus loved the rodeo and beer.

"Yeah. Paul arrived and they're renewing their friendship with lots of toasts back at the Paulina Tavern," explained John, as he kindly poured the amber liquid into each cup. I rarely drank but, parched with thirst, I gulped mine down and smacked my lips, holding out my cup for more. Well, fancy that, I thought. Warm beer was wonderful. Hadn't eaten a thing and the beer had a comfortable feel in my stomach.

"Hell, the tavern is where I should be," Pop mumbled, shifting from cheek to cheek. "Jane! My rear is ready for a change of scenery. Let's go!" Just then, Paige returned with the girls.

"Not really a hygienic place," she said. "Flies were on everything. Didn't think the girls should eat it." The little girls were on the verge of whining when we all heard laughing, youthful voices bubbling up from the arena as kids their ages chased twelve greased and unhappy baby pigs. This event held the attention of my nieces for another five whole minutes before they began their complaints of boredom and hunger once again. My sister knew they needed to leave, too.

"We're going to the Paulina Store," she announced. "The girls need snacks."

Mom and Pop, interested in exploring the Paulina Tavern and trying out the cushiony bar seats, followed my sister. She'd seen enough blood and guts for the day. John left too, saying it was about time to check on Angus. Phil assured all of them we'd meet them in a half hour or so when the rodeo ended.

Now that we were alone, Phil said to me, "Kristy, you've got a silly grin."

"I do?" I said, puzzled. "Oh! The beer!"

"Are you tipsy? 'Cause we should head back to Paulina to check on your dad." I nodded at both question and statement. Phil steered me to the car because the ground was wavy.

"Phil," I said. "Don't be scared but I think we're having an earthquake." Phil smiled at me.

We arrived to the screaming sound of a pickup's engine revving up. My head thumped painfully. We parked in front of the Paulina Store. Phil stood next to John Sheehan and Angus. My dad was inside his new Ford pickup, gunning the engine like a wild man.

"I think it's the commencer," Dad hollered.

Phil and John shouted back at him to stop pushing the motor because he'd ruin the truck. Dad ignored them and stayed bent over the steering wheel, likely because of a few whiskeys with his drinking pal, Angus. Angus had an innocent, contented look as he hugged his bottle of Johnnie Walker. My sister kept nervously patting the heads of my nieces who laughed and pointed at their funny grandfather. Mom and Pop sat on a bench munching ice cream cones.

Near our car, we saw a group of four or five Wrangler-clad cowboys and ranchers—the former with the new clothes, the latter in their much-washed Sunday best, slouched against the old dance hall. They contributed to the mayhem with their own economical remarks.

"That's jest like a Ford," drawled a liquored-up cowboy. "They always need attention."

Holding up the same wall, a pot-bellied rancher, clearly offended, jerked his head around to the speaker. "Whet are yew talkin' about?"

"Ah'm sayin' a Chevy would treat a man better 'n thet."

61

"Oh, stick it in yur ear yew dumb Chevy lover."

"Whut wus thet?"

Without a word of warning, a skinny fist shot out and connected to a pudgy jowl. A blurred mix of arms and legs started pounding down on hat-covered heads while spurred boots kicked at knees or stomped bare hands as they fell as one lump into a writhing pile.

Similar to a tennis match, the audience turned away from my dad and concentrated on the real pastime of choice— a fight!

Black smoke poured out from under the hood, and a raucous grinding noise rose above the escalating smacks and growls of the battlers. I saw heads from the crowd jerk back to my dad. He'd successfully blown up his motor. He rolled out of the door without a backward glance, and he and Angus staggered John Wayne-like towards the tavern with the now peaceable combatants close behind.

Feeling puny from the tepid beer, I couldn't have cared less. I struggled out of the car and stood against it, unnoticed. I spotted my reflection in the side mirror. Large wisps of hair stuck out sideways from my braids. The piping of the car seat had imprinted on my face.

Wondering if this rodeo day had any redeeming qualities left, I heard a quiet tenor behind me.

"Whar've yew bin all mah life?" it croaked. A scrawny teenage boy in full cowboy garb stood looking at me with twinkling eyes and open grin. Me. Hung over, bedraggled, and married me.

Oh yeah. This day was definitely worth keeping.

ᏜᏜᏜ

Funerals

It was 1975 on the ranch and Dad was in trouble already. He was drinking hard and not eating. He'd stop for a while and take care of business but start his deadly lifestyle all over again. Anger and frustration came between us most of the time and, although we still loved each other, it was buried underneath his alcoholism. But on occasion, because of a dreadful situation, love couldn't help but rise to the top.

"Finn Sloan died last night," said Phil, walking into the kitchen. "He was on his tractor working at their Black Powder Camp and had a heart attack — guess he was diabetic. Forty-two-years old. Funeral's on Saturday."

"We should go. Finn was one of the first people to introduce himself to us," I said. "Dad will want to attend, also."

On the day of Finn's funeral, Dad was stone sober. The little church in John Day couldn't hold one more person. Many families had to stand outside and listen. The faces of young and old revealed their shock. People weren't supposed to die until they were old and sick, having already lived a rich, full life. We all sat and listened to the elderly preacher talk about Finn, while the Sloan family cried behind a black curtain.

A darkness came over me, as if something heavy was sitting on my chest; it felt like a strangling claustrophobia coupled with an impending doom. *Snap out of it, Kristy,* I told myself. *Stop the dramatics and think of the pain and loss of Finn's poor family. You dope.*

After the service, people drifted reluctantly out of the church as if their departure made the death too final. The peculiar feeling followed me outside. Phil, Dad, and I stood on the sidewalk. Dad knew most of the people, but Phil and I were still new to the country to start up conversations, so we kept to ourselves. Shane and his brother Noel Gallagher from Izee walked over. After Dad introduced us, Phil and I stayed in the background while they discussed weather, cattle, and hunting—the favorite subjects of ranchers.

Without realizing it, tears poured down my cheeks as I watched my dad visit with the neighbors. The Gallagher brothers broke off to seek their wives, and I moved to Dad's side and grabbed his arm. As soon as I did, I was wracked with sobs, and they wouldn't stop. Phil and Dad looked at me, concerned. It was unusual for me to cry. Anger was more my thing.

"What's wrong, honey?" Dad asked me. "You barely knew Finn."

More sobbing prevented me from answering him. I clung to him and didn't want to let him go. His shirt became wet as I buried my head in his chest to hide my tears from the mourners.

"Phil," said Dad. "Why don't you take her to the Wagoneer. There are a couple of people I have to talk to."

As Phil walked with me back to the car, I could not stop crying. "What's wrong?" Phil kept asking. "This can't be only about Finn."

Inside the car, it took a while before I could talk.

"You're right," I told him. "It was about Dad. It's as if I'm mourning *his* death. It's coming hard like a freight train, and I can't stop it. He doesn't listen when I beg him to stop drinking. If he doesn't, he'll die. He thinks he's invincible."

Two grueling years later, at age fifty, Dad was gone. It was too soon.

***

In the early seventies when we arrived in Izee, it seemed that an entire generation of older ranchers was dying off. Phil's mom and dad sat with us at Louie Martin's funeral. Again, as with Finn, the church was packed and spilled out onto the sidewalk and street. Louie was an icon in Izee as was most of that generation. Phoebe Sloan, whose dad died recently, and her friend Dolly Swanson sat in the rows in front of us. The priest seemed a lively sort. This young Father was temporarily officiating while the regular, elderly priest was on sabbatical.

"We have come together to honor the life of Lonnie Martin," said the priest, walking over to the casket.

BAM!! His hand came down hard on the casket. People jumped and squeaked. "He was a good old boy!" continued the priest. "We know he loved God!" BAM!! Babies whimpered.

"And Luthor would want all of you to do the same!" BAM!! A low, irritated murmur started up among the mourners.

Beside me, Pop said in his best non-whisper, "This guy should be in the movies."

"Now," the Father continued, relentlessly, "everyone think about how we loved the deceased as we listen to the lovely voice of Barbie Walley."

The song was pretty and she had a good voice, but the temperature inside the church was too warm and I nodded off. Through my foggy doze, I heard the priest carry on about the blood and body of Christ. He offered

Communion to all who cared to partake which only included three or four souls.

Pop snorted awake beside me. "What's going on now?" he said aloud during a lull in the priest's delivery. Communion ended, and the priest popped a wafer in his mouth and lifted the goblet, the size of a toilet bowl, and drank its abundant remaining wine in big, slurpy gulps.

"Boy," Pop didn't whisper, "he sure loves his wine!"

In front of us, Phoebe and Dolly's shoulders were shaking. I glanced around seeing faces turn our way — some glaring, some smiling. I leaned over to Phil and mouthed, "Can we trade places?"

"Are you kidding?"

***

Then there was the non-funeral which, it turns out, was the more common occurrence in our family history. This was the cremation where, somehow, the ashes ended up missing or lost. This time it was my mom, who died from a long illness and far away from home.

As usual, during horrific times, things are bound to get confusing. Mom wanted to be in the Izee cemetery next to Dad, and we needed her ashes. My sis and brother-in-law took care of Mom's stuff and, at the time, had put everything in a storage unit in Los Angeles — the only thing to do at the time. One of those things was Mom's ashes.

A few months later, I got a phone call. "Kristy," said my sister, Paige, calling from Los Angeles, "the storage unit was broken into, and Mom's ashes are gone."

"What?" I asked, not sure if I'd heard her right. "Paige, what dope would steal a person's ashes?"

"Desperate ones, evidently."

I was horrified. Some idiot brute stole Mom's ashes! "But why ashes?" I said, dimly. "Who would want ashes?"

"Well, they didn't just take ashes," said my sis, with extraordinary patience. "They stole guitars, amplifiers, and other stuff they could sell. Something about Mom's urn drew them, I guess."

"Oh, right. I see," I said, slightly mollified. "Probably threw them in the trash when they opened it up. Poor Mom." Like it made a difference to Mom after she was gone. What was she going to do? Rise up and haunt everyone like the butcher's wife Sarah in *Fiddler on the Roof*? *"Tell me that it isn't true and I shouldn't worry . . ."* she sang.

For a year or two we bemoaned Mom's fate, figuring her remains were part of the human detritus in a Los Angeles dump. During this time, the funeral home contacted us saying that the previous owner had cremated and then mixed their clients' ashes together to save money—then gave the families urns filled with a composite of strangers' ashes. Sort of like a disgusting fruit smoothie but without the liquid. Those funeral folks eventually went to jail or were heavily fined for their actions. By this time, we'd not only lost Mom's ashes but then discovered her remains had been mixed up with who knows who.

Then one summer day, after another couple of years went by, my brother-in-law showed up at our door. "Got something for you, Kristy," he said. "Found it under a bunch of stuff when I cleaned out the storage unit." From behind his back, he brought out a small urn.

"Oh my gosh!" I said. "Mom?"

He nodded. "Evidently they weren't taken," he said. "The thieves just piled stuff over it when looking for valuables. Also found out they are really hers and that the funeral home did the mixing of ashes after your mom was already cremated."

The whole episode made me *mugwumpy*, but then the humor part of my brain kicked in. One of the most important attributes my mom and dad bequeathed me was humor and irony. Mom would have *loved* this.

ᏽᏽᏽ

Ranch Baby Showers and Births

In Izee, baby showers and births were as numerous as weddings. Or, the other way around, one hopes. The Izee women folk invited me to all of them. I always felt clueless about what to get a baby. It took a while, but I eventually caught on.

So the first invitation to a baby shower arrived. Baby gifts were as mystifying to me as, well, babies. Phil wasn't being unkind but honestly thought they resembled tiny hairless monkeys. An opinion secretly held by many men. And maybe a few women, too. Anyway, I had to shop.

The baby aisle at Chester's grocery store was immense. The baby stuff didn't look that interesting, plus I still had no idea what babies needed. Powders, lotions, nose cleaners, ear cleaners, eye cleaners, diapers, weird mouth plugs, all shapes of bottles, breast pumps (Yikes!), onesies, twosies, threesies, rubber teething items, and other sundries. Nothing struck me as fun.

The dog aisle was better. Maybe a tiny, rawhide chew? A jingle ball? A stuffed antler moose hat? Dog brush for tangled hair? Nah, babies don't have much hair. The potty-training spray could be useful but, as I leaned in to grab it, a random thought occurred to me: a gift appropriate for a dog would not make me a popular neighbor. *So what?* Throwing caution to the winds, I grabbed it anyway and bought it.

The following week, I arrived at the shower for Amy's baby girl and found fifteen women chatting and giggling in Angus and Ethel Sheehan's living room. A pitchy pine log burned in their brick fireplace. On a library table, covered with a snow white tablecloth, sat a punch bowl, silver coffee pot, mixed nuts, and six or seven kinds of homemade cookies. *Phil is going to be so envious.* I started loading up, but then saw no one else taking a plate of food, so I stuck mine back. Evidently it was gift-opening time.

Close observation was primary, because to me, this was new territory.

With Amy on my left and Gwen on my right, gifts were opened and passed around the circle. Amy's sister, Jules, wrote in a small book after

Amy ripped open each package. The group *oohed* and *aahed* over each gift, even a rectal thermometer.

"Would you look at that?" said the elderly lady in a red cardigan and print dress. "A breast pump. Wish we'd had one when I had my babies."

"Lovely burp-up blanket," said another mother. "I remember when my Lacey spit up all over my Carhart jacket. Never noticed it because it was during calving and already had bits of afterbirth and calf poop on it."

Amy stopped opening gifts, whipped out her breast, and put her newborn, Bronwyn, on it. After a few minutes of baby slurping noises and a patting/burping moment, Amy turned to me. "Would you like to hold her, Kristy?" she said. Not waiting, she handed over Bronwyn to me.

I blanched. "Well, uh, of course! Heck, I wondered when you'd ask. I've been patiently waiting the whole time, you know." I held tiny Bronwyn on my lap, and jiggled my leg a bit. Amy was opening my gift.

"Oooooh, how...different," Amy said, trying to get enthused. "Potty Training Spray—for dogs."

Dead silence filled the room.

"Neat, huh?" I said. "It should work on babies, as well, don't you think?"

Suddenly a noise like rats drowning in a mud puddle emitted from the babe.

"Oh! She pooped on you," someone said. "Hahahaha. You're officially an Izee woman now, because a baby born from Izee has christened you."

"Can you hand me that spray, please?" I asked.

So many babies were born the first years we lived in Izee that I decided it would be more affordable and original to make baby moccasins. Also, it seemed the mothers, though nice about it, weren't sure my early gifts were beneficial for babies.

At the next baby shower, I settled down on an ottoman at Gunnar and Etta Sloan's home. This time the shower was for Gwen Sheehan. I checked out the gifts once again: quilts, pillows, teething rings, cowboy boots, shirts, t-shirts, socks, sippy cups, colorful mobiles. Not a dog gift among them, which was a tragic oversight, I thought, even though I had given up getting dog gifts for babies. No more tiny rawhide chewies for Izee newborns.

Then came my gift. I held my breath.

"White doe hide moccasins with wings?" Gwen smiled. "Adorable."

All around the room the ladies gushed, yes, gushed over the mocs. Through the years, I made the mocs with the angel wings, green leaves,

68

antlers (all from soft doe), sheep's wool, and elk. At last I'd found my baby gift.

***

Swoozie and I had already shared one baby event, when I was trapped between her pre-birth breasts in a closet-size dressing room. Now she wanted me to attend her and Jake's birth of their first baby. It was an honor to be invited, and the parents-to-be had it all planned. They'd call when Swoozie went into the hospital. Because it takes an hour to drive in, I'd have to leave the second they called. No matter what.

And so I did. The music CD blared out Wagner's *Ride of the Valkyries* on the way to the birthing—a perfect selection for the trip in to John Day and the Blue Mountain Hospital. A birth represented all the beauty of being a woman. Swoozie's family had its origins in Sweden, so she, like my paternal Scandinavian relations, was also Valkyrie material. I parked and took the stairs two at a time to Swoozie's floor. There, Dr. Gifford was pacing in front of her room.

"Nothing yet, Kristy," he said. The doc was our G.P, too. "Waiting for her to dilate more. She's close, though."

I let out a huge sigh. I could hear Jake and Swoozie's mom, May, inside the room, talking in low voices.

Dr. Gifford turned to me. "She's cat-napping between contractions."

"Oh," I said, "that's good, since Swoozie has cats."

Doctor Gifford looked at me, unsure if he heard right. Then he grinned. "Oh, good one, Kristy. Sort of."

"Can't help it," I explained. "Jokes pour from me during stressful, non-violent events."

"UHHHHH!" Swoozie cried out. Dr. Gifford disappeared into the room.

"Another one's coming," Jake said. "Hang on Swoozie. Remember your breathing."

"The baby's coming," Dr. Gifford said. "Push now, Swoozie."

"Oh honey! Baby," said May, distraught to see her only daughter in distress. May held a video camera, but it shook so hard the film would be a blurry mess.

I came in after Jake motioned to me. Swoozie's voice gained volume.

"You want me to take over filming, May?" I asked her, since she was filming the ceiling.

"No, no," she said. "I'll do it. OH MY LORD! WHAT'S THAT?" The camera pointed at the nurse's bottom.

"It's the baby's head," said Dr. Gifford. "She's crowning."

69

"Let me film, May," I said. "Then you can watch for the baby easier." I reached for the camera and May pulled back. I lunged and grabbed it while it filmed our shoes scuffling around.

"NO!" hollered May. "I HAVE TO DO THIS!"

Swoozie sat up to look and saw May's camera skill going to hell.

"MOM!" Swoozie bellowed. "LET KRISTY DO IT!"

I snatched the camera, gently shoved May toward the birthing spot, and stood next to her. I managed to focus on the spot just as the babe popped out. A sweet baby girl lay on the table extension, wiggling with the umbilical cord still attached to Swoozie. May and I hugged. We hugged Jake and began to hug the hospital staff, including the janitor in the hall, when all hell broke loose, again.

A nurse gasped. "Doctor—" she whispered.

Something scary was happening.

"Everybody out," said Dr. Gifford. "Now."

We looked at one another, fright mirrored on our faces as we retreated. Swoozie's door closed behind us. No one said a word. Fifteen minutes later, the staff finally came out and said all was well. The umbilical cord had prematurely separated from Swoozie and she was in danger of hemorrhaging, but they fixed it.

Hugging resumed. This time as we went en masse toward the janitor he must have thought we resembled the zombies in *Night of the Living Dead* because he dropped his wet mop and walked away fast, slipping and sliding down the hall.

"Humph," I said. "What got him all a twitter?" Our group seemed benign until I looked around at the others. Our clothes were askew, hair stuck straight up and out, glasses smudged, and our eyes were bloodshot.

On the road home, I felt honored and blessed to have been asked to be in the birthing room, and my life changed a little for the better because of it. I also considered the difference between calving and a human baby's birth. As wonderful as it was, Jake and Swoozie's birthing left me a trembly wreck.

Give me a calving any day of the week.

ॐॐॐ

Dancing, Weddings, and Breasts

We were at a dance when he caught my eye. I stole that line from the song "Blame it on the Bossa Nova," but it was true. The only difference was that my girlfriend had caught Phil's eye, and he asked *her* to dance. She already had a boyfriend so, since I stood next to her (sort of a beauty and the beast scenario), he asked me. On the dance floor of my hoity-toity girl's school, Phil did the latest dance, The Jerk, and I knew he was for me because this sixteen-year-old boy could move. So could I. Or, at least *I* thought so.

Never said I was a *good* dancer, but I loved to dance. When I was seven years old, I watched American Bandstand. Everyday. The Pennsylvania teenagers danced the Mashed Potato, the Monkey, Hully-Gully, Watusi, the Chicken, the Fly, the Pony, the Twist, and later, the Jerk and the Surf. Free-style was popular when I met Phil. We thought slow dancing was not challenging enough for our vast repertoire of innovative, yet slightly odd, and maybe disturbing, moves. When we came to Izee, the only place to dance was weddings. We were responsible for embarrassing many a young couple. The amazing thing was that people kept inviting us. Maybe we were the entertainment factor.

***

In the tin mailbox was a big cream envelope with embossed gold printing. "Phil," I said. "Tank Mallory is getting married and we're invited. Do you think they'll have dancing?"

Phil looked up from his Zane Grey book. "Likely western swing…," he said, a trifle grumbly. "We probably won't even remember how to dance."

"Nah," I told him. "It's like riding a horse, you never . . .oh, wait a minute. Wrong cliché for me, since I'm not good at riding a horse. Besides, where's my man who did the Jerk and melted my heart?"

"Phumblemigacherf." Phil's focus shifted back to his book.

A month later, we gussied up, which meant I wore a dress and Phil wore his best Levis, a western shirt, a tan cowboy hat, and shiny black cowboy boots. Except for the wedding party, male attire would resemble Phil's.

71

We arrived right before the ceremony. In the church we saw a cluster of brown, black, and tan cowboy hats and women with hairstyles sporting the same colors. Quickly we nestled into an end pew just as the wedding march started. As if a silent command occurred, like a dog whistle to a dog, all the cowboy hats came off. The ceremony was quick and the couple darling. Two hours later, a disk jockey set up his equipment, and the dance floor was cleared. The obligatory dance of the bride, groom, and their respective mothers and fathers, went off without a hitch. Then the D.J. got busy.

The first song was fast and an oldie, "Johnny B. Goode" by Chuck Berry. Phil grabbed my hand, and we jumped onto the dance floor.

"C'mon," he said, sliding into position. "This is a promising beginning."

We were on fire; our arms and legs flying around. Soon other couples, mostly younger, joined us but stayed a safe distance away. Oblivious of my surroundings, I'd already nailed another dancer right in the kisser. Luckily she'd dipped into the spiked wedding punch and didn't notice.

Next tune up was "New Orleans" by Gary U.S Bonds, so we stayed for more crazy gyrations. After the fifth song, Phil noticed little kids lining up beside him, making the same motions he did. He watched them as he went up on his toes during "Chain, Chain, Chain," by Aretha Franklin. Little feet followed him perfectly. Transitioning into a modified twist when Joey Dee and the Starliters' "Peppermint Twist" blasted out, the kids didn't blink but shifted as smoothly as their mentor, Phil, with the new movements.

A big guy danced over to Phil. "My kid's following your every move, Phil," said Tom Sand, a logger and rancher from Bear Valley. "They'll probably be showing me your dance styles when we get home."

"They're game, alright," Phil said. "Perfect mimics."

"Think I'll have them teach me!" said Jeff, dancing near us. "I've never seen anyone dance like you and Kristy. What dances are they?"

"Haven't a clue, really," Phil said. "When we dance, anything can happen—basically we're out of control, sort of like a Ouija Board, only not evil."

Ike and Tina Turner singing "Rollin' on the River" exploded from the DJ's amplifier. We were on it like a duck on a bug. I channeled Tina while Phil and his small tribe moved back and forth to the beat behind me.

"Oh man," I puffed. "I wish I had Tina's shimmy-dress!" Tina's style was a fast shimmy and strut so I made it mine. Phil and his troupe, The Philettes, followed. Before we knew it, the dance was over. The Philettes

72

dispersed to their families with many congratulatory pats on their heads. We limped home happy.

"It's been *soooo* long since we danced that hard," I said. "Can't wait for the next wedding, if…er, we're invited. Some folks looked at us like they worried about our mental health or the fact that they lived too close to us as neighbors."

"Nah," said Phil, grinning. "They're just jealous of our phenomenal dancing."

"Yeah, probably," I said. "But didn't you think there was a lot of whispering and pointing going on?"

***

Our next wedding invitation appeared in summer. My dress was a straight, fairy-light batiste, but emphasized my non-ample chest. I looked through a Victoria's Secret catalog and spied some latex inserts. I ordered the smallest, which would make my negative size twins normal size. The special rubber squished when squeezed and felt soft, like a real breast. Phil liked them.

At the wedding, after the vows and the meal, a four-tiered white and lavender cake held the regal position on the dessert table. The newlyweds cut into it, smearing each other with cake and frosting. Cameras flashed and the cake was cut for all to enjoy.

I was first in line. The first thing I love about weddings is dancing. The second is wedding cake. It always tastes fabulous. This beautiful cake was covered generously with thick glorious white frosting, and I absconded with two pieces that had life-sized, piped sugar flowers on them. What? Nobody asked me if the second piece was also mine, so what of it? Jeez.

"Hope it cools down before the dancing starts," I said to Phil, while happily munching my second piece of wedding cake. "The falsies are sticky with sweat already."

Phil removed his jacket and walked over to the cake table and back. "Is that your second helping?" he asked. "They wouldn't give me a slice. Said I already had one."

"Huh? My second? *Nooo.* The caterers are being hard-nosed. What's their problem, anyway? Humph."

A pounding beat on a piano came over the speakers: "Great Balls of Fire!"

"We're dancin'!" Phil said.

I took a huge bite of cake and met him on the dance floor. For two hours we hardly left the dance area, because every song was good, fast,

73

and old. All the elements needed for a great time. I felt movement on my chest a couple of times but was too busy to care.

Suddenly, the party was over and folks lined up to throw rice as the couple ducked into a limousine and drove off.

"Have fun!" I shouted with the rest of the crowd. "What a night."

Goodbyes and hugging started among the guests. I was grabbed by a young neighbor and swept into a friendly bear hug. He let go, stepped back with a puzzled look, and mumbled, "Nice to see you," and left.

"That was weird," I told Phil. "Do I have cake all over my mouth or something?" I'd managed to snatch a goodbye piece the size of a plate before the caterers whisked it away with an alarmed look on their faces.

"Yeah," he said, "but I doubt that's why Sean seemed perplexed. Did you accidentally pinch his rear or something? Since you're his dad's age, it might have disturbed him."

"No, not that I remember. But that would be disturbing all right." I shook my head while trying to figure it out.

Back in our hotel room, I caught my image in the mirror as I walked to the bathroom. I saw three distinct breasts. One of the falsies had escaped from my padded bra and found a home in the middle. I wanted to call the kid and explain.

"What would you tell him?" asked Phil, horror-struck. "'Uh, my rubber breast traveled while I danced, blah, blah, blah.' It's bad enough he felt it when you hugged, but to actually discuss your breasts with a teenage boy? No, it's best to let sleeping breasts lie."

ᏋᏋᏋᏋ

DINING OUT

*After weeks of beans and taters, even a change to
taters and beans is good.*

~Anonymous

Born but to banquet, and to drain the bowl.

~Homer—Odyssey

Local Restaurants and Public Bathrooms

From our tiny freezer, the venison steaks stared back at me. Yeah, it was good to have meat. Hawkeye or Chingachgook wouldn't complain. Neither would Zane Grey's characters. Probably not John Wayne, either. But deer meat gets tiresome. Restaurant food called to me. So, Phil, Dad, and I headed for John Day. Dad had been telling us about a legendary restaurant called *Sofie's*.

Sofie's restaurant was stuffed with loggers, ranchers, cowboy ranch hands, mill workers, wives, babies, and a dog or two roaming around the room. The place smelled like our grandparents' house during the holidays, igniting heaps of memories of warm, yeasty bread, cinnamon, and onions. The room was narrow and long, with booths along the west wall and a counter and swivel stools running the along the side of the east wall. We lucked out and found a booth that was soon emptied—and not because we stood next to the booth, drooling and ballsy-staring at the occupants.

Waitresses, young and old, flitted from table to table, balancing trays loaded with a king's feast. Plates contained hash browns, meat (choice of beef, elk, deer, sheep, chicken, or pork) including prairie oysters, volleyball size sourdough biscuits, stacks of pancakes, toast, eggs, and three jellies and three jams—and that was the diet plate. Regular-size breakfasts held twice as much, with oatmeal on the side, and coffee. At Sofie's, an individual order could have fed Paul Bunyan *and* his ox.

"Isn't this a great place, honey?" Dad asked me. "Breakfast here keeps you satisfied for two days, and the biggest order is only two bucks. After a meal here, I have to let my belt out a notch."

The menu had heft and was as big as a traffic sign. "I'll have the smallest breakfast choice," I said to our waitress, a pretty girl flushed pink from rushing around. "Where's the bathroom?"

I followed her pointing finger to the back. I noticed only one door and it said Bathroom. Not male or female. One of the older waitresses came by, and I asked if there was a 'Ladies' room.

"Nope. Don't know no ladies. HAHAHA!" She smiled. "Hi I'm Sofie! And I didn't have enough money to put in two, so this is both." I smiled back and headed for the two-in-one. Just as my hand hit the knob, the door opened and out popped a grizzled, sawdust-covered logger.

"Beg yur pardon, ma'am." Bits of fragrant pine fell off him as he walked away. Inside the room, a tiny hook was the only lock and the hook was loose. When locked, a half-inch gap still showed if the door was nudged a little. I turned around and went back to the table. I'd wait until I got back home.

My breakfast had mountains of everything. I plowed through most of it and still had a doggie bag for the rest. Phil and Dad finished all of theirs. At home, I ate mine for three days, and each meal was a logger's-sized portion. It was excellent food—all ten or twelve different starchy carbohydrates of it. Carbohydrates are my favorite nutrient and obviously popular with others in Grant County. Made me feel like a native.

***

Then there was the *Horizon Restaurant*, part of a motel. This restaurant was bigger, with more tables and booths. Our first dining experience at the Horizon happened during the Grant County Fair. Mom was visiting the ranch, so we all came in to see the fair, rodeo, and parade. Phil went to the bathroom this time. The door was shut, so he knocked and the door swung open. The room had no separate cubicles. A pudgy, florid fellow sat on the pot.

"Gosh," Phil said, embarrassed for the guy. "Sorry, didn't know anyone was in here—door wasn't latched."

"Yeah," the man said. "Hasn't locked for years. No problem. Sorry about the smell. Almost done here."

Phil backed out and shut the door as tight as he could and came back to the booth. Before the food came, Phil made another trip to the back hoping it was empty this time. The door was ajar, so he decided it must be empty and pushed on in. Another man was in there this time, hunched over the sink. Closer inspection revealed a boy, tall and gangly, dressed in rodeo garb. Tight Levis, fitted aqua shirt with pearl-headed snaps, black cowboy boots, a belt with **ADAM** tooled in the back and a huge silver buckle in front. His black hat lay upside down on the toilet lid. Blood smeared the sink, faucets, and the guy's shirt and face. He looked up as Phil pushed in.

"Oh heck," said Phil. "I'm sorry! The door wasn't completely shut."

"Blood all over my hands and pouring out my doze so couldn't close it," the kid said, his voice muffled like he had a cold. "Fight in de parking lot — I lost. Heh-heh. God I love fair time."

Phil's stomach started churning as he backed out and returned to the booth. The three of us munched away on cheesy mountainous omelets,

77

homemade hash browns, thick ham slices, and fresh orange juice. Phil looked at our food and turned green. The waitress passed nearby.

"Could I just have dry toast and coffee, please?" Phil asked. "Not feeling so hot."

***

The third eatery in town was known for its beefsteaks. Thick steaks, from cattle raised locally, ruled the menu. The *Smokin' Gun* was always dark. The bar was in the back. It had pool tables, where people played every hour the establishment was open. A back door opened into an alley for the bar patrons. On the street front, the restaurant was available all day for families. In town for supplies on a Saturday, Phil and I came in for lunch. Inevitably voices from the bar, along with cigarette smoke, drifted out to the restaurant.

"I tol' Lonnie, look that *#/% tree over before your first cut! Is it leanin'? Is there another ^*%#* tree in its path when it falls? Do you have an escape route in case it comes back on you? If you need to run, *drop your saw* — don't take it 'cause it'll drag you down. But he's a good #^!*^ kid and he'll do fine. If he listens."

"Your */<*## shot, Georgie!" said a cheery voice. "Better pay attention or I'll *%#! cheat on ya!"

A tiny waitress came to take our order. "Hi, she said in a high sweet voice. "Our lunch specials today are rib eye steak with baked potato, rice, corn, and macaroni and cheese. Lasagne made with fresh ground steak, potato salad, and cheese soup. The desserts are chocolate pie with chocolate sprinkles and real whipped cream, coconut pie with real whipped cream, lemon meringue with real whipped cream rather than egg white frosting, chocolate cake made with mayonnaise and cream cheese frosting, and red velvet cake topped with red shortening frosting and cream cheese layers. What would you like today, hon?" she asked, looking at me.

"I'll have your first special, a coke, and a piece of red velvet cake. Can I get that a la mode, please?" I weighed 102 pounds.

"Why sure! And you, darlin'?"

"I'll have the second special, a beer, the lemon pie, and coffee with cream." Phil weighed 144 and was also underweight. We were Lilliputians, and we ate everything right down to the parsley.

"Is my turn ta !#^*pay for lunch, Georgie!"

"Nuh uh," replied the second man. "Ya bought ta ^*@##*> drinks."

"Thes' okay, yur ma is ma fren'. Ah wan' ta doit."

"Nope...'s said 'n done — Wahs s'rong?"

78

From the dining room we heard an alarming, wet, regurgitating sound.

"Aw, man! George! Ugh. Ah ain't payin' fer *tha'!*"

***

The fourth restaurant was in a small town halfway between John Day and Canyon City. We hadn't eaten there before, but it looked homey, like the food held promise. Phil, Wade, and I slid into a booth. The waitress brought the menus and left. Their plastic covers had some kind of dark brown smeary stuff on them. With one finger we opened them—also grimy inside. The print was almost obliterated.

"I gotta go to the bathroom so bad!" Phil said. "Be right back."

Wade looked down at his fork. Attached was a long crusty hair with something that looked like a scab hanging off the end. We looked at each other, our eyes pregnant with the question: was it or wasn't it?

Phil returned. "The restrooms aren't great," he said. "Someone got sick in there, and no one has cleaned it up. No soap, either." Wade showed him the fork.

"Maybe we should try," Phil suggested.

So we looked at the menus and decided on our food, just as the waitress came back. At the same time, the cook sauntered out smoking a cigarette, with an inch of ash still attached. She started to cough, a thick phlegmy sound, into a stained handkerchief and hacked up something. She opened the cloth and examined its new contents, with the cigarette ash conveniently falling in there, too.

"Whadoyawant?" asked the waitress.

"Um…we'll have three small coffees to go please," Phil told her.

☾☾☾

Paulina Tavern and Beer on the Range

Phil and Wade were traveling east on the Prineville Paulina Highway, heading for home. The summer heat made the inside of the International Scout scorching. Especially since it had no air conditioning. The ranch was still an hour away—too far to wait for a cold drink. Paulina was only ten miles up the road, and it seemed like a good place to stop. Preferably for a couple of icy beers.

Phil pulled up outside the Paulina Tavern, drooling with the anticipation of a nice drink. As the sun disappeared behind the juniper-dotted, high-desert hills, a cacophonous racket blew out the windows and door. Phil and Wade looked at each other.

"What on earth was *that*?" said Phil. "Are Banshees indigenous to eastern Oregon?"

"What's a band sheet?"

"No," Phil said, "a *Banshee*. You know, the mythical Irish fairy woman who screeches when someone's gonna die?"

Wade looked at him. "Wha—? Are you sayin' we're gonna die just 'cause we want a beer?"

"No, no. Never mind." More howling sprinkled with loud laughter almost drowned out Phil's reply.

"So, wanta go in?" asked Phil. "It's gonna be cooler for sure—besides, it'll be a bathroom stop, too."

Wade's eyes got big. "Uh, no, I'm kinda sleepy." he said. "Just bring me out a beer."

Phil noticed all the pickups parked around as he walked into the tavern. His eyes adjusted to the dark inside while he carefully avoided bumping into people to reach the bar. The mirror behind the old bar revealed only women behind him. Well, he thought, at least I can *see* their images so I know they aren't vampires.

"Hi, Alvin," said Phil, "I'm glad to see a familiar face. Could I have two bottles of beer?"

"Hi, Phil," he said looking apologetic. "You sure?"

Women started yelling behind Phil. "Give him his beers in a bag, HAHAHAHAHA!"

"Put 'em in a sack, Alvin! HAW! HAW! HAW!"

Phil felt a pressure behind him as the women squeezed closer. "That's fine, Alvin," he said. "I don't mind if they're in a sack." Gales of screaming laughter and ribald comments bordering on the profane showed their approval of Phil's choice.

"Er . . . I'll just go to the bathroom, real quick," Phil told Alvin. "Be right back." He edged away from the bar, taking baby steps so as not to awaken a slavering beast, but the women followed like tigers stalking their prey. Five feet from the door, Phil leaped into the tiny bathroom, not looking behind him. His need to use the toilet evaporated when the ladies pounded on the door like Jack Nicholson in *The Shining*. Phil could have sworn he heard, "Little pig, little pig, let me in . . ." He looked around and saw a tiny window five feet off the ground where only a ferret could squeeze through, if the ferret ever found itself in a bar. Suddenly the pounding stopped.

"Phil?" asked Alvin. "Come on out. I'll walk you to the bar."

A feeling of gratefulness washed through Phil's being. He started to open the door then remembered that some of the women had deep voices. He almost broke one of the fear monger's golden rules: Number 2. ALWAYS verify identification.

"How do I know it's you?" Phil yelled. "Gimme a sign!"

"Okay," said Alvin, sighing. "Your father-in-law, Paul, owes me $30,000 dollars he borrowed last year."

Phil opened the door. Alvin put his arm around Phil and walked him through the restless mob, which parted just an inch away from them, and then closed in behind them. Disturbing murmurs surrounded the men. At the bar, the shouting started up again.

"Give him two beers in a sack! Two beers in a sack!"

Alvin got out two cold ones, opened them up, and poured them into a paper sack.

Phil stared at the bartender. "I trusted you, Alvin, or should I say, *traitor*?"

The gals went nuts with laughing and applauding.

"Sorry, Phil," said Alvin. "Men aren't allowed in because it's Ladies' Night. They get what they want, and if they don't...well...you see what can happen. And, they'd turn on me. Now leave. Run as fast as you can—"

But Alvin didn't need to tell him twice. Phil was out the door, handed the sack through the window to Wade, locked all the car doors, and took off.

81

Wade peeked in the sack. "What the—? Where are the beers? What was all the screaming and hollering in there? "

Phil looked at Wade with crazy, bloodshot eyes. "Those are it," said Phil. "You can go back there and get some if you want, while I stay out in the locked car, and wait."

"No. I'm good."

***

Summer was halfway over when Phil and Wade helped Rafe move the Izee Ranch cattle to the Lonesome pasture on their Malheur Forest permit. Before they started, Wade discovered his saddle strap was chewed in half and barely holding together. He drove back to the ranch and got another saddle and also four beers, which he stuck in the creek back at the forest. The scattered timber didn't provide much cover, so the heat was brutal.

After three hours of inhaling dust and shuffling slowly behind the cows and calves, the tired men turned the horses toward the creek. Another of Izee Ranch's young hired men, Lex, veered off earlier to bring in some stragglers. Phil, Rafe, and Wade drank their beers while he was gone. When Lex rode close with the three or four laggards, Wade jumped on his horse to help Lex bring them in to join the rest of the herd.

"Wade told me he has a beer waiting for me. I'm parched," Lex said. "It's a crazy hot day." He and Wade got their horses and Wade dropped down near Phil and Rafe. Lex headed to the creek, bent down, and grabbed the last beer.

"Heeeey!" he said. "This bottle's been opened. There's mud in it!" He glanced at the guys. Rafe looked horrifed.

"It's a helluva thing to tell a man there's a cold beer coming," said Rafe, "and the man finds an open bottle with mud in it! Good gawd almighty! Here. Take mine."

"Aw, no boss," said Lex. "I can't take your beer."

"C'mon. Take it!"

Turning red with embarrassment, Lex snatched it up and guzzled it down.

"You know," continued Rafe, his mouth twitching a little, "it's also a helluva thing when your boss gives his ice cold beer to his hired man." His eyes twinkled. He stared straight at Lex and grinned.

"Oh," said Lex. "You've already had yours. This one's mine, huh? I get it. Play a joke on the city kid who works hard in the hot sun all day."

"Har, har, har! I sure had you, heh boy?" Rafe said. "You should see your face, Lex! Happy, sad, confused, and relieved all within a couple of seconds! Gawd that's rich!"

Lex stared at him.

"C'mon, son," said Rafe, his voice softened a bit. "Now you're one of the guys. You gotta take it in stride and teasing's part of it. Okay? Besides, just think of the story you can take back to San Francisco. You can even call me a *sonofabitch*."

And with that, Lex smiled big.

♋♋♋

RANCH ACTIVITIES

Humour is by far the most significant
activity of the human brain.
~ Edward De Bono

You will do foolish things, but do them with enthusiasm.
~ Collette

Mating

I rushed into the shop, pushing the door so hard it clanged against the wall. "Phil, something's wrong with Frodo!"

Perched on a tall stool, hunched over his workbench like a hip vulture, Phil held a fine-tipped paintbrush over a delicate design on a leather wall piece. He managed to keep the black ink away from the leather when his arm jerked wildly.

"Kristy, calm down," he said. "I almost ruined this piece!"

"First he attacked Jane by jumping on her," I hurried on, "then he let out a high squeal and flopped over. Jane looks fine, in fact, she's preening. But Frodo looks dead."

Phil stared at me. Together we ran out the door to the rabbit hutch.

As we watched, Frodo resurrected himself and jumped on the other female, Dart. A convulsion gripped him while on top of her then he shrieked and fell over. Dart started grooming herself.

"This is far-fetched," I said. "But what if this rabbit weirdness is a Ying-Yangish-Karmic-Hari Krishna punishment because we named the females after our mothers?" A recent phone call to our moms informed them about their namesakes. Phil's mom stuttered," Oh! Well, I guess that's nice?" Mine laughed.

"We better call Nita," Phil said. "It might be rabbit rabies. Didn't rabbits carry the bubonic plague in France, or was that a scene from *Monty Python*?"

"Phil," I said. "Remember Nita's warnings: if any harm came to them, we'd never again get to taste her buttery herb bread. Although I think she smiled when she said that."

While deciding whether to risk telling Nita, we noticed Frodo doing it again. Attack, seizure, scream, and fall off. We watched, gathering research and analyzing the data before calling our friend. Sure, other people might misinterpret this observational technique as a peculiar, even slightly unhealthy use of one's time, but Nita required details.

She loved her animals, so we weren't keen on telling her the rabbits had psychotic fits or narcolepsy. Or that they might be morphing into goo creatures similar to the Siberian huskies in the movie, *The Thing*. In the film, the monster ate the dogs and then their heads shot willy-nilly out of its chest, snarling and snapping. Phil's usual good sense omitted my theory when he talked to Nita.

Nita cut to the chase. "Does he mount them?"

"*Mount* them?"

"Yeah, you know, to mate."

"Oh! That's what he's doing! But he screams."

"Uh, huh, males do that," she said. "If you keep them together, he won't leave them alone."

Phil chuckled.

Nita didn't think it was funny. She believed in good animal husbandry. She also packed a .357 pistol to protect her brood when she fed them.

"Phil," she said. "Fido won't stop and could die."

"Frodo," Phil said, correcting her, surprised everyone hadn't read Tolkien's stories by now. "You know, like in *The Lord of the Rings*?"

"Is that a story about wrestling?"

"No—He could *die* from fooling around?" said Phil. "What animal does that?"

"Well, female black widows kill the males after sex, don't they? Leave them together and see for yourself."

With that, Nita hung up.

The next couple of days, ignoring our leather work, we loitered near the rabbits' cage. We didn't have television.

Observing the bunnies proved hard work. We studied them for a week—taking turns to sleep, eat, or go to the bathroom. We'd put Frodo in with his wives then back out, giving them all a short break. Sadly, we misjudged his endurance when, after jumping on Dart, uttering a final weak squeal and flopping off her, Frodo didn't wake up.

The girls looked out from their cages, and their liquid rabbit eyes accused us *Why? Why? Please get us another fella!* However, it was not to be. We'd ignored Nita's advice, killed Frodo, so Dart and Jane were returned to Nita.

Later we learned a happy bit of news: Jane and Dart had scads of children fathered by a succession of husbands. We called our moms to reassure them about their namesakes. Each didn't say much. In fact, for some reason they changed the subject and hung up prematurely, but not before mumbling words like *unwholesome curiosity* or *peeping toms* or *where did I go wrong?*

***

86

In the city, people spay their cats and dogs. They don't want FiFi mating with Butch in front of God and everyone which, for some reason, dogs seemed to do. On the ranch in our yard, animals make love mostly when ranchers stop to chat with Phil and he's gone.

When Lance, a young, too handsome neighbor, drove up, I walked out to greet him and his blue heeler, Jasper. Fat, my female dog, came, too. She'd just finished her heat. But even before greetings were exchanged, Jasper leaped on Fat who, swear to God, smiled. In seconds, the dogs were wriggling and panting between us. Trying to ignore them, I gently nudged at them with my foot but they still managed to hookup. Surprisingly, Fat sort of babbled during the performance. So did I.

"Well, Lance, how goes the calving?"

Oooooooo, yip, yip, owww, eeowe, whooooo.

"Fair to middlin' I s'pose. Can't complain."

"Be nice to get it over with, huh?"—not only referring to the cows.

Ahhhyeee, arrff, whooff.

The two lovebirds were attached bottom to bottom. This dog-love-attachment situation was a first for me, making it difficult to keep track of the conversation.

Jasper panted hard, as Fat critiqued his performance with more noisy yips and howls.

Pointing to the green hills, I desperately tried drawing Lance's attention away from the dogs.

"COULD THE GRASSES GET ANY GREENER UP THERE, LANCE?" I shouted above the dog din. "SOON THE COWS WILL FIND IT AND GET GOOD FEED, RIGHT?"

The shouting caused Fat to yowl louder, probably mistaking my strident voice as an invitation to sing together. The dogs always howled with me in sort of a pack choir.

Luckily, Lance wasn't bothered at all and instead offered his views on grasses and grazing while I worked hard at not being a voyeur. After the brief conversation with Lance along with Fat's contributions in the background, Lance and Jasper (now unattached from Fat) hit the road.

"If she has pups, I want one. I'm sorta partial to talkin' dogs, though it's the first time I've heard one talk during mating."

You're not the only one, I thought.

***

After the rabbit incident, Nita gave us another chance, with only slight hassling, bestowing two geese upon us, a male and a female.

"This is a no-brainer," she said. "Don't let me down, okay?"

"Of course we won't. The rabbit thing was a mishap. Geese are a whole different story."

She looked long and hard at us, like if she focused her power, we might change our crazy ways and do it right this time.

The gander, Biter, soon ruled his outside domain. Showing off for his lady goose, he attacked everyone, always coming from behind to pinch legs. His neck stretched and his beak snapped as he rushed at his prey getting in a nip or two. Phil and Wade took to carrying long pliers and swinging it behind them as they walked.

When spring arrived, the geese wandered too far, and Biter came back one evening without his mate. For weeks, he babbled and moaned, calling for her.

It was Nita time.

"He needs a female," she said. "Don't have one. You'll have to ask around. Get one soon. I gotta get off and feed the goats. They're eating my laundry." Never any long conversations with Nita.

Ranch chores took precedence over finding Biter a new wife. A few days later, we looked out the window. A beautiful Canadian female goose stood near Biter.

Mememememurmurmee. She cooed tender promises to him. Once again, our leather work had to wait while we watched Biter and his wild girl. Days passed as the wild goose took off flying above him, dipping down close enticing and cajoling—daring him. On the ground, he started following underneath her, watching and honking as she circled. Before long, he waddled fast and flapped his wings. Rising, just a little bit off the ground, but without altitude or skill, he smacked, repeatedly, into barbed wire fences, posts, trees, horses. The wild goose watched and waited. So did we, but we were spent from laughing so hard. Each time he crashed, he wobbled crazily back to a starting position and tried again.

Finally, one sunny morning we looked out the kitchen window, just in time to see him navigate smoothly above everything—tickled we didn't miss his perfect solo flight. Beside him, in sync, was his wild goose mate. Honking, they circled the house once and disappeared forever.

The saying *love is in the air* now made more sense.

ᏕᏕᏕ

Fish and Other Wet Things

It was Phil's second trip to Izee, and this time he was going fishing.
No messing around looking in old ranch sheds or at rusty farm-hay
equipment. Phil grabbed his fishing pole, flung himself out of the car door,
and was hoofing it down Poison Creek Road toward the South Fork before
Mom turned off her Toyota.

Phil, a fisherman in his mother's womb, knew the July weather kept
the river low, so the fish hid deeper in the undercuts to stay cool. So, ten
feet from the water, he eased to the ground and slithered toward the bank
in case fish could see his silhouette. He didn't want to screw up his first
Izee fish encounter, so he Navy-Sealed it. No amateurish T-rex plodding
along, shaking the ground. The lush jungle of hemlock, bullrushes, cattails,
and Reed Canary grass pressed at his face as he inched closer.

Before he ventured a peek, he dabbed some mud on his cheeks—
minimizing detection. He lifted his head slowly over the water. . .

"Oh, jeez!!" Phil crabbed backwards, abandoning all caution in the
heat of the moment. "Tha— tha— that's a TROUT!" His heart paddled
wildly, and all his parts tingled. He cast his line as silently as possible and
let his grasshopper-baited hook float into the water's hidey holes. "It's like
this river hasn't tasted a lure in a long time," he whispered, reverently, not
bothered at all that the trout didn't take his hook. "This is a *virgin* river."
While he worked to still his heart, the bulky shape blatantly stole his
hopper.

"WOW!" he yelled at the river. "*O mahny pahdme hum, o mahny
pahdme hum,*" experiencing a hippie moment and remembering the
Roshi's calming chant.

"My precious!" he said casting a second fat grasshopper through the
air. Plop.

After thirty seconds, another long figure headed up towards it, getting
bigger, and bigger, and bigger.

"A SHARK TROUT!" Phil gurgled. "What in the name of the Holy
Mary's hairy mole is that?" The gliding leviathan barely lipped the
surface, executing a taunting swim-by. In the little eddy, the fish made its
own wave. Once more Phil willed his body to settle down. He stared at the

89

rippling water, wondering if he had gotten sun stroke, or just a plain old stroke—maybe as a consequence of all that secondhand marijuana smoke we'd encountered at hippie parties, and it was finally catching up to him. He decided to sneak another look to make sure he was sane. A small cloud overhead kept the reflection muted as little by little he leaned over the bank. Fish eyes stared back, briefly, oh so briefly, and then they were gone again.

The fishing line floated by and jerked *down*. Phil played it cool.

"That's right, sucker," Phil whispered. "Taste the green goodness of the grasshopper."

Phil felt the tiny nibblings and minuscule tugs but held firm. Waiting…waiting.

BAM! The river monster pulled hard and took off with its prize. Phil let it run. Let it feel secure entering into its cavernous home. Phil did nothing to prevent the hook from gouging deep into fish flesh. The pole bent nearly double as the fish charged back and forth in the depths of the pool. Eventually it tired. Its open mouth emerged above water. Phil stopped breathing and gawked as he wound the reel lever. This was an *old-man-and-the-sea fish*. A God of the Upper South Fork of the John Day River. A trout respected and revered in its domain. This fat emperor trout had to measure at least 26" tail to nose. A trophy. Phil's first trout out of the South Fork.

So he kept him. Couldn't help it.

But, Phil promised this fish that if he had any say in ranch things, the future would be catch and release, so he could raise these freshwater Goliaths like a herd of choice cows or big-horned bucks. Phil hoped, with a little care and attention, the trout would stay abundant. And, not only the trout, but other water and land/water inhabitants . . .

***

Not all river critters are slimy with gills. Our dogs, Dollie and Rizzo, and I found that out on a riverside jog one morning in May. We followed a dirt cow path etched into the meadow along the south side riparian fence. The dogs padded ahead, hoping to jump a fat rodent in the surrounding tall grass. The South Fork, thirty feet away, ran fast and deep from the snow melting in the headwaters of the forest.

A mile and a quarter passed under the old Nikes, and a .22 caliber semi-automatic pistol slapped against my right hip. Izee air, at ten a.m., caressed and cooled. In May, the weather could be cold or hot, changing from one day to the next. Today, shorts and a sports tank was the exercise attire.

While thinking of the chores to be done at home after the run, a strange noise reached me, even above the rushing sound of the water.

GAH*SCHNIFF.*

Was that a dog sneeze? It was nearby and sounded like it came from the river. The water ran closer to this part of the fence. I stopped and looked around for the dogs. Maybe one of their noses dipped into some fuzz stuck on a willow?

"Girls," I yelled. "Where are you two?"

Something moved way out in front of the path. Two pairs of furry dog ears, one brown set and one black, bounced up and down in the grass, too far in front for the sneezy noise.

GAH*SCHNIFFLE.* GAH*SCHNIFFLE.*

The noise had a soggy, moist sound. It came from the river. A beaver? Then something caught my eye because it was floating but not moving downriver. I scanned the water's edge. Two wet heads with ears and twinkly black eyes appeared. *Otters!* They were agitated and warning me away. Luckily the dogs weren't close enough to notice.

GAH*SCHNIFF,* GAH*SCHNIFF,* blew out of the two black noses.

I've loved otters ever since I saw a science show where two otters floated on their back holding hands. I wanted Phil to see.

"Oh great," he said. "They're trout-eating machines. We'll have to live-trap the otters and take them to another place. Let's go."

Not exactly the response I expected.

But they were gone. A couple of days later, Phil checked again and the otters had returned.

"They got pretty excited and kept spitting at me," Phil said, laughing now that he'd seen them. "If I got too close they'd make a snurffly sort of sound while dog-paddling to keep their eye on me. I've got to get a picture of them." Of course, the two disappeared by the time Phil got back.

Like the famous mythological Selkies, it was probably best since they could have been beautiful maidens disguised as seals (or, in this case, otters) ready to steal Phil away. As much as Phil loved water, he might not put up a fight, either. Just in case, I kept my eye on him, making sure the river's lure didn't pull him too often.

It was difficult. In the first years, he spent all his free time (and lots of not-so-free-time) on its grassy shores. The river, in turn, revealed its coexistence with implausible critters— like rattlesnakes.

One hot summer day, while Phil and Wade were mending the fence next to the river, they decided to cool off in the water; but on the way, they were interrupted by a buzzing in the tall grass.

"These snakes are *everywhere*," said Phil, after chopping the snake's head off with a shovel. "I almost stepped on this one. The second snake today."

"Well, it's summer," Wade said, "and Snake Den Ridge is just across the highway. They're thick this year."

On the spur of the moment and for no good reason, Phil decided to throw the snake in the water. As they approached the bank, they saw movement on a large flat rock sticking up out in the middle of the stream. Coiled on it was a huge rattler.

"Look at that!" said Wade.

From the river's edge, Wade started flinging rocks at the snake until it slithered into the water, straight at them.

"Eeee!" they squealed in unison. It was the mouse situation all over again.

"Back up!" Phil yelled. "BACK UP!"

"You back up!" The high, thick grass tripped them and they went down.

"Where'd it go? WHERE DID IT GO?" Both scrambled toward a gravelly spot. Phil noticed he still clutched the dead snake and flung it into the river near a deep sluggish pool.

While they watched, a hefty trout rose from the depths, circled the snake, nudged it, and disappeared back into the darkness. It came back up one more time before withdrawing forever.

The guys stood with their mouths open.

"Have you ever—?"

"No, never," said Phil.

"—seen snake-sniffing trout or rattlers that swim?" said Phil.

"Nope. But I don't want to swim here anymore," said Wade.

ᏬᏬᏬ

Trespassers

In Lake Oswego, we lived on a lot one-third the size of a tennis court, so we never worried about trespassers, just the occasional peeping tom, psycho mailman, or drugged-out neighbors.

Four thousand acres changed things. Two miles of the south fork of the John Day River and surrounding hills hid living things, whispering to passersby like the sirens of Odysseus's sailors: *Come . . . come stranger. . . I'm a plump trout waiting for your hook. Or, here am I, a wild beast...hunt me . . . you can brag to your mates about my big horns and how easy I was to find and kill.* Okay, that's a bit Tolkeinesque but not far-fetched. Something about Izee, maybe an enchantment, compels people of all ages to trespass.

Trespassers snuck in everywhere, especially during hunting and fishing season, so Phil started sheriff-ing the ranch. At first, he was friendly and calm.

"Hello!" Phil shouted, smiling up at a hunter coming off the hill on Snake Den inside our fence. "Thought you should know that you're on our land. Just a friendly reminder, we don't allow hunting."

"I wasn't *hunting* deer, just observing. Heck, I loved that deer movie, Bambo." The guy shifted the strap of his 30-30 rifle further up his shoulder. "I thought this was public access."

Behind him, nailed onto a juniper, hung a big-lettered "**NO TRESPASSING PRIVATE PROPERTY**" sign. He leaned against the tree and continued babbling. "If ranchers put signs where they could be seen, you guys wouldn't have trespassers — especially if it can't be seen from the road. So, if I'm on your land, and I'm not saying I am, then this is your fault, not mine."

Phil looked pointedly at the sign then at the hunter.

"All right then," said the hunter. "Good afternoon." Without another word, the guy scampered over our barbed wire fence, leaving skin and a piece of Pendleton wool hooked on it. A mud-splattered rig of road hunters screeched up and retrieved their friend, who flung himself through the gaping door. Gravel exploded as they took off but not before Phil got their license plate number.

Later that day, Phil rode Sandy up the same hill and found beer cans and a buck hanging from a juniper. Phil rode home and called Marshall, the game cop. Marshall tracked down the hunters, and over time, the men paid a hefty fine.

The encounter made Phil grumpy, particularly when my nephew came into our house and told us his own incident.

Earlier in the day, as Wade hunted along Poison Creek, he wiggled on his belly towards a four-point buck resting beneath a juniper. The wind blew against his face, so he knew the animal didn't smell him. He positioned for a shot, ready to squeeze off a round, when the buck burst out from its bed and bounded away.

"Oooowee," spoke a stranger, walking up behind Wade. "Man, that buck was HUGE! I'd been watching him a while, too."

Wade jerked around. "Where the hell did you come from?" he asked. "This is private property."

"I walked down a draw that had old cars half-buried in the dirt, and it's okay, I have permission from the owner. I'm a distant cousin. We visited recently, and he told me I could hunt."

"A cousin on whose side?" asked Wade. "The Larsons or the Shaws?"

"Uh. . . um. . . the Shaws."

"HAH! Wrong—"

"I meant Larsons!"

"There is no Larson or Shaw; my grandfather owns this place."

"What's his name?"

"Paul Timm."

"Yep, that's him. My long-lost cousin."

As Wade finished his story, Phil started grinding his teeth. Damn trespassers!

***

Every deer and elk season brought new incidents. Some hunters were creative. Phil decided to travel up and down the road checking for road hunters or rigs parked with nobody in them. So, when the next season opened up, he wasn't surprised when he discovered a new Ford pickup parked behind the Izee Ranch hay barn. Our land and fence run behind their building. The rig was empty so Phil waited. Soon four hikers, soaked in bloody clothes, appeared, carrying an impressive deer head. Each man held a beer. Phil started to speak, but they could see he was angry, so the hunters interrupted him and started talking at the same time.

"—oh, hey! This isn't our buck; we found this head in the hands of trespassers and ran them off for you!"

94

"—sure, this looks bad, but this buck was already crippled so we put 'im out of his misery."

"—do you mind if we keep it? My doctor told me that venison is good for my enlarged prostate."

"—we shot this buck on the National Forest, and it jumped your border fence so we had to track and kill him. We were on our way to ask your permission to retrieve it when Joe here remembered he has to be in bed by six o'clock, so we decided we better finish before he keeled over."

These guys got points (so to speak) for originality, but we turned them in anyway. If we didn't, word could spread that this ranch was easy on trespassers.

***

Trespassers that fish, for some reason, behave badly when discovered on private land. Their credo seemed to be: *You don't own the fish in the river, by god!*

The best hidey spot for sneak-in fishing is the west end of the ranch, where the river is closest to the road. The dense brush and bunch grasses stand four to five feet high. We've lost cows, neighbors, and sometimes tractors in there for years at a time. It's called the *Izee Triangle*. Locals and strangers think it's an urban myth. No one knows about it but us Izeeers. Izeeans. Izees. Oh to hell with it.

It's in a blind spot from the house. This is where the trespassing fisherman loves to throw in a hook. Phil discovered a whole family there one day. A young couple and three little kids. Oddly, they were in Sunday clothes like they'd been to church. Parents and children each had a pole hanging over the water. Phil pulled his truck over and walked down the grassy bank. Five somber faces turned and looked at him. The dad had a net lying next to a creel stuffed with trout. "

"Kids, this here is a kind and gentle man," the gaunt man said in a low monotone. "You can see in his eyes he's filled with generosity."

Phil looked behind him wondering to whom the man was referring. "Uh, sorry," Phil said. "There's no fishing allowed here."

All their gloomy eyes locked onto Phil. The sun went behind the clouds turning the day cold and dark. Phil felt his neck hair rise against his Levi shirt.

"It's not even fishing season," he told the *Addams' Family* while trying to remember a protection spell from *Bewitched*. "You could get in trouble fishing out of season."

Rain poured from the sky, drenching the odd group. They didn't flinch but kept staring at Phil as, one by one, with measured movements, they gathered their gear (Eye of Newt, Tongue of Asp, Toe of Slug, if they had toes) and slithered up to their car and drove away. Phil shook his head thinking, *Man it's good I don't have television, but if I did, I'd never watch another scary program.*

***

After a particularly trying fishing season of abusive trespassers, Phil took to mumbling and sputtering. Once in a while, he'd shout a word at nobody. Was this Tourette's? A chemical altering in his brain because of the toxins we used daily in our leatherwork?

"Phil," I asked him one day, unable to put it off any longer. "Have you been smoking mushrooms? I noticed all the little mushrooms that sprout from horse and cow poop nearby are gone. If you are, you know how I feel about hallucinogens."

"What? Who's Lucy Engines? Isn't that a Beatle's song? What about her?"

"You're scaring the cats. The dogs run off yipping, and the chickens have stopped laying."

"Okay, it's this trespassing thing. Today, driving down the road, I see a sedan parked at the Izee Triangle. Of course, I look and see nobody. The grass must be six feet high there. I'd already had two go-rounds with people who were unreasonably nasty. One guy sicced his little daughter on me, and she bit me. I was in no mood for diplomacy. So I slog my way into the brush and find an elderly couple fishing."

"What do ya want?" said the tiny shrunken man, with a remarkable resemblance to Yoda in *Star Wars*. "Get the hell outta here. You're scaring the fish, idiot!"

"Sir," I said," this is private land."

"Don't sass me boy! I drove log trucks through here from the Johnson Mill when your mama was cleanin' spit-up off your baby chin!"

Then the little old woman joined in. "You better stop attacking my husband!"

"She came for me, swinging her pole like a Samurai and screaming 'Stand still and take it like a man. How dare you think you know about this place! We've fished here for fifty years!' The pole just missed my nose. Good Lord! Where did this little woman, who's probably ninety, get her strength?"

"Kristy, they chased me up the bank and into the pickup," Phil said. "After that, I decided to let them stay. And it wasn't because I was scared of them. Really."

Feeding in Winter

Tululah's heavy-lidded brown eyes opened. Her long chestnut curls lay over the pillow. A few strands stuck to her moist bare breasts. Channing's earthy man-smell lingered on the cotton sheets. She ran her delicate hands reverently, slowly over his side of the bed. It was still warm. What happened last night? Tululah tried to remember. Then a rush of heat spread over her body, especially down her belly and even lower—

"KRISTY!" Phil hollered, "You're heading for the ditch!" Jerked into the present, the romance novel tumbled down onto the muddy floor. I yanked the truck away just in time from going into the dry river bed.

"AAAAH!" Phil yelled. "Are you trying to kill me?"

"SORRY!"

I looked back and Phil was getting up from the ground. Uh oh. He came to the window. His hair askew and glasses crooked. His hair looked good messy. Even with hay in it.

"You knocked me clean off the truck!" His eyes looked down at the floor. I moved my leg to hide the paperback, but he'd already spied it. "Is that a book? Were you *reading*?"

"Um... .no? Yes."

"Didn't we agree that it's not a good idea to read while driving the hay truck?"

"We did?"

"Yes! Remember when I tumbled off the back, and both Rizzo and Dollie did a nosedive, landing on top of me?"

Oh, it was memorable all right. In the middle of a steamy love scene between Lucinda and Shep on the veranda, the hay truck ran into Poison Creek. It got stuck in the mud, and Phil had to bring the little crawler to pull it out. I played dumb.

"Wasn't that a dream? Are you sure it happened? Didn't it have warty, horned gargoyles chasing us trying to get the dogs? Since gargoyles aren't real, it sounds more like a dream."

He just stared long and hard at me, then turned and climbed back on the truck bed. I behaved for a few weeks.

Sometimes Phil, rather than I, drove the truck to the feeding area. Mainly because he couldn't explain exactly where he wanted to feed the cows. It usually went something like this:

"You know the rock that resembles Abraham Lincoln with the dead moss for his beard?" said Phil. "Next to it, is the mound of dirt with the cow skull on top and a clump of tall wolfy rye grass—"

Or: "Let's go to the crook in the river where Number 10 calved a few years ago, and you had that infected hangnail, and Rizzo barked at the coyote she saw on the hill—"

His frustration, while trying to get me to understand, grew to the point where he ended up sputtering at me, and that's when he'd decide to drive to the exact spot he wanted. Especially when I'd respond with:

"What rock? What dirt pile? Which calf of Number 10's? Didn't we ship number 10 twenty years ago? Which crook of the river? There are lots of crookish bends in the South Fork."   Maybe I'm wrong, but men have developed their own method of direction when hunting critters. Many times I've heard Phil and other guys say stuff like, "You'll be on stand at the gray rock that sits to the left of the four-foot juniper with five berries hanging off it. You know the place?" "Oh yeah. And Wade stubbed his toe there in 1980 while glassing for bull elk in Soda, right?"

In fact, guys usually just say a couple of words and they understand each other.

"Five berried juniper—?"

"Stubbed toe—?"

"Yep. Later."

***

Feeding started in the morning, and the hungry cows came to meet us before we got to Phil's special spots, so he had to drive through them. He'd drive fast, and I worried about running over the calves.

"Watch out for that baby, brake! BRAKE! Oh no!! I'm pretty sure you ran over it. Now it's a puddle of calf squish. What's the use of raising calves if we keep running over them?"

"No, I didn't," he said. "And we haven't run one down yet. They always get out of the way."

I leaned out the window, looking back to where the little quivering body lay covered in blood—but wait. No body. The calf popped up and started nursing its mom. False alarm. This time. We were lucky, that's all.

It's always a scary, chancy thing because the cows jostle each other for the first bites of choice hay as it comes off the truck bed, while their babies try to stay close. Some ranchers feed alone and use an automatic transmission. Some wedge a stick between the seat and the gas pedal, or their truck idles high, and it enables them to jump off and on their hay wagon. It's sort of every man (and cow) for himself. Obviously this technique is only effective on straight stretches, but Phil and I'd watch Jeff Gallagher feed that way, and we puckered up constantly, worrying about him and the cows.

So back to our feeding and my driving. Our hay truck had a stick shift, so the clutch and my left foot got a good workout to maintain a leisurely, even pace; but it still idled too fast in first gear for me to not pay attention. I drove riding the clutch.

When the snow was deep enough to cushion Phil or the dogs and the calves hadn't arrived yet, I could read and drive with abandon. Once again, bad Kristy emerged. The reasoning behind the relapse was (and this is a pitiable excuse) radio station reception drifted in and out, so I got restless and bored. I'd grab my latest paperback.

Charlie's massive fist smashed into Monte's jaw. Monte staggered, his six-foot-five frame absorbing the blow. He jumped on the Sheriff's back causing them to fall onto the bed of pine needles. Drusilla cried out, "Don't hurt him. I love him." "You cannot love a Campbell; it is forbidden!" said Charlie, panting fast. "I warn you, blackherd. Stay away from my betrothed or you will be filleted in front of her when next the moon is round."

"Hah! Too late, sire," laughed Sir Monte. "She carries my blossoming seed in her belly! It was easy to entice her into my bed. Her luscious breasts responded as I—"

"COULD YOU GO FASTER?" Phil shouted. "THESE BALES ARE SO DRY, IT'S HARD TO KEEP THEM FROM BREAKING UP AND SLIDING OFF."

Guilty and caught red-handed, my hands jerked up and the book toppled behind the seat.

The truck inched along at one mile an hour while I leaned over the seat trying to find the book. The cows passed me. I retrieved the book and then the wheel. Phil stood in front of the truck to get my attention. He'd gotten off, walked passed my window, and planted himself.

"Honey," he said, once again coming to the window. Phil's window visits always meant I may be in trouble. "Why can't you go faster?"

"The cows. It's terrifying, thinking that a cow might get run over."

"They'll get out of the way, I promise."

"How do you know they'll move in time?" I asked. "Are you God or something?" But he'd already disappeared, getting back on the truck. Why was I always so mouthy, always having the last word? The man was a saint.

***

During the four months of the year when we did the morning feedings, on the way to where Phil dropped the feed, our small talk never varied: "Phil," I said. "Number 26 looks funny."

"Could you be more specific?"

"Just have a feeling," I said. "She's not eating, and she's too skinny. Hasn't she calved?"

Phil drew out a tiny notepad and flipped through the pages. "Yep," he said, "and I saw her eating yesterday. She just spends more time with her calf than on the feedline. She's a second calver."

"There's Number 5," I'd point to our favorite cow, a Hereford. "A sweet-natured thing."

"Yes," Phil agreed. "She's the last one left from our original herd of ten pregnant heifers." He could scratch her head, and she'd never move away. She liked his touch.

"There's Number 13," I continued. "Will her babies grow up mean like her, do you think?"

"Depends," Phil said. "Not as a rule."

"How much snow fell last night do you suppose?"

"At least a foot. Feels cold, so it'll clear tonight and drop."

And so on. We'd become Izeers. This repetitive small talk, worrying about cows, calves, and neighbors, was almost scripted and happened nearly every morning. Like a comfortable soft blanket we could depend on. And the disagreements served a similar function—checks and balances of stewardship, of life on the ranch.

ᏊᏊᏊ

ANIMALS

I go about looking at horses and cattle. They eat grass,
make love, work when they have to, bear their young.
I am sick with envy of them.
~Sherwood Anderson

I have been studying the traits and dispositions of the
"lower animals" (so called) and contrasting them with the traits
and dispositions of man. I find the result humiliating to me.
~Mark Twain, Letters from the Earth, 1907

Squirrelly Cows

Ranchers aren't foolhardy. And most cows do have easy dispositions. But then there are the squirrelly ones—like on sorting day, when the calves are separated from their mothers.

As I swung up onto the rotting post, the longhorn cow swiped her pearly horn at my backside. Even her breeze screamed fury as she veered away from the gate.

"Kristy, hold your ground," Phil bellowed from behind a thick dust cloud created from the dozen milling animals, "or we'll never get these cows separated from their calves." Only his white teeth kept him visible.

"Sorry. Can't take floating teeth seriously," I yelled back. "They may not even be *your* choppers. Who's president of the United States?"

"Two pairs are coming," Phil said. "Make sure the calves go through— *not* the cows. Pay attention."

I mimicked Phil under my breath. It's hard to do a proper mimic when terrified. The lead mother put her head down, horns directed at my heart.

"HAH!" She saw arms waving madly, a jumping impediment making loud sounds. "GET AWAY. HAH!" Only she probably heard, "BLAH BLAHTITY. BLAH!" Then she charged, and her impediment vanished. Phil stomped towards the impediment, now perched on the fence and hugging the fat post.

"This just isn't working. If you don't stay on the ground and move the gate to sort them, we'll be here all night."

"Yeah, but their nostrils snort fire and their horns grow pointy. Even if they do have nice hairdos." That's something I've always admired. Cows' hairdos.

A rumbling vehicle drowned out my whining.

"Oh look," I said. "A pickup is pulling in. Someone is interrupting the fun." A short, wiry man with a handsome grin jumped from the truck, followed by three brawny boys, all with the same grin but taller than their dad by a foot.

"Need help?" he shouted. "My boys and I can pitch in." It was Rog Morgan with sons, Trev, Logan, and Lonnie. Plucky folks from Paulina, always doing things no one would attempt. The family was famous.

"Go on home, Kristy," Phil whispered. "Don't feel bad. Not everyone is as fearless as the Morgan men." Before Phil finished the last word, I was on the path to the house, waving to my replacements.

An hour later, Phil walked into our kitchen.

"Sorry I was a coward," I told him. "The horns are scary."

Phil chuckled.

"No really," I assured him. "Next time will be different."

"If I hadn't seen it—" he said. "Who'd a thought?"

"What?" I said. "Who?" I felt like I was part of an Abbott and Costello act.

"You won't believe it."

"Why? C'mon. Try me."

"Okay." Phil let the drama build. "When the longhorns came close to the Morgan guys, they jumped onto the fence. Every time."

***

It's no wonder. Cows weigh 900 pounds and can inflict serious injuries, for gosh sakes. That's easy to forget when working cows. Especially in corrals.

The Madisons, our neighbors and intrepid cattle folk, asked us to help them work cattle, which involved corral work. Phil helped in the corrals, and I stood near Nancy, outside the corrals, mostly gossiping and watching. Cole Madison, Will and Nancy's grown son, worked the alley shooing their pregnant cow to Phil. Phil waited inside a small round holding pen that had smooth, high sides.

"Here she comes," Cole shouted. "Heads up, Phil."

"Ready," Phil yelled. "Oh — Jeez — Get back! Aaahhh!" Cole jumped over rails to reach Phil, just as the cow rammed Phil repeatedly against the panel with her head. Luckily she was hornless, but Phil was trapped. Cole threw open the gate and hot-shotted her until she trotted out, shaking her head in anger.

"Gosh I'm sorry, Phil," Cole said. "I forgot to warn you. She's nasty."

That night, I looked at Phil's wound. A red and purple, tray-sized bruise blossomed across his back and side. I expected to see Jesus or maybe Elvis, which made me wonder, why Jesus and Elvis all the time? Why not Marlon Brando or John the Baptist?

"Phil, this bruise is gigantic. Better go to the doctor."

"Nah," he said, "It'll heal."

It did, but it turned yellow, purple and green. Fortunately, no Elvis or Jesus appeared, or we'd have had a sort of Graceland/Holy Land pilgrimage situation and our house was too small.

103

Sometimes a cow's inner *Cujo* appears during the ear-tagging of her newborn. Three techniques may be used. The first technique is a fat-chance scenario shown in *BEEF Magazine* where a handsome man (Phil or Tom Selleck) grins at the camera while punching a tag into a sleeping calf's fuzzy ear. The calf is smiling. The mother watches with a gentle expression on her face.

The second technique (highly favored) is tricky. Phil catches a running calf by hooking its leg with an aluminum pole-hook and then hands me the pole. Phil kneels on the calf and punctures its ear with a numbered tag and if Jupiter aligns with Mars, we're gone in sixty seconds.

The third, and least-preferred tagging method, was invented in the heat of battle by Phil. Our evil cow, Number 13, was the reason for this technique. It is called "the hook-the-calf's-leg-and-pull-it-up-onto-the-back-of-the-truck technique while keeping an eye peeled for the mother." To this day, many ranchers have eyes that rove in opposite directions because of using this technique.

This method was created in stages, beginning when Number 13's *first* calf woke up during the tagging and squalled when the tag was punched in. Thirteen's head shot up from the line of cows on the fresh hay two hundred yards away. She galloped over, snuffled her calf thoroughly, and gave us a look.

"She's an excellent mother," said Phil. "That's good."

With that charitable assumption in mind, the next year our brother-in-law Jim helped us tag calves. When Phil grabbed the leg of Number 13's calf, it sent out a screech. The cow, grazing on the feed line, made 400 feet in ten seconds. She towered over her calf and halfheartedly rushed the guys.

"She looks mad," Phil said, backing up. "So let's hook the calf, haul it up, and tag it. Kristy, drive next to it." I drove the truck between 13 and her calf to give the guys time to get on.

"She's coming!" Phil shouted. "Get up! Get up!"

Number 13 charged. Phil and Jim scrambled onto the flatbed with the dogs. Jim barely made it in time. He bonked the cow's head with a shovel. The dogs snapped at her nose and ears. Using her head, she rammed our Carter dog, Rizzo, into a corner trying to crush her. The dogs decided to jump off the truck. Number 13 went for them as they scooted under the truck tossing barks over their shoulders. I opened the door to help, but she wheeled and came for me, like the shark in *Jaws* but without the creepy music.

"Kristy, NO! Stay in!"

I scrambled back in and rolled onto my back. She forced her massive head and shoulders into the cab so the door wouldn't shut.

I kicked at her head. "EEK… EEEK…!" She backed out, shaking her head and bellowing. I yanked the door shut.

"Phil," Jim said, gasping hard like Big Jim in *Wild Kingdom* when the grizzly ran him up a tree. "She wants to kill us."

"Tomorrow." Phil nodded, solemnly. "Things will be different."

The next day, I drove as Phil and Jim, hands steady, rode on the back and stared ahead. Hook and shovel ready. *The Magnificent Seven* score played in my head as I maneuvered casually into the herd between Number 13 and her baby. Phil made the grab.

"Got him," Phil whispered. ". . .*Uh oh.*"

Number 13 exploded, circling the truck, screaming threats in cow language and banging her head around in angry frustration.

"She's coming!" Jim hollered while helping pull up the calf. "Watch out!"

Crazed with fury, the cow jumped halfway onto the truck bed swinging her head in a sweep, her teeth clacking. Her tongue stretched out, resembling a striking rattler rather than a quadruped's cold-cut my mom used to put in sandwiches. Her eyes bugged out like golf balls.

"Jim!" Phil hollered, scooting the calf all over the metal surface away from the mother while attempting to tag its ear. "Keep her away!"

"Right," Jim answered, clunking 13's head with the pitchfork. The cow's snapping teeth just grazed Jim's unprotected ankle and instead chomped the pitchfork's handle into two bits just as Phil snapped the tag on.

"I'm lowering the calf down the other side now," Phil whispered.

In a blink, Number 13 was there, mouth wide, wanting Phil's face for supper. The calf wriggled over the side. Phil spidered backwards, knocking Jim then himself off the truck bed. They squealed in harmony as they fell onto the grass then scrambled over each other to join the dogs.

"We're okay, Kristy!" said Phil. "It's over."

"Kristy?" Phil repeated.

Slapstick never before seemed funny. Finally, I got it.

ᏊᏊᏊ

Poignant Horse and Dog Stuff

The kitchen window in our tiny house was like a theater. I'd wash dishes and gaze at outside vistas that were always diverse. Maybe Phil was doing chores, or the dogs playing, or the horses nibbling on the lush Kentucky blue grass. Horse watching was a delight of ranch life, even though the horses mostly stood and fed. I liked horses and wanted them to be safe and healthy. But all living things, including horses, have stuff happen to them.

On this particular day, I watched and noticed one of Pop's horses, Red, drop his head but not to eat the grass. He was more like a baby who gets so sleepy its head falls. We'd observe the horse for a while to rule out obvious things like maybe it was just a normal behavior of this horse. We just weren't sure enough to be worried. But one day, as I watched, it got weird enough to alarm me.

"Phil!" I said. "Red is acting strange. He closes his eyes, moves his head like a bobble-head toy, then drops his head and buckles his knees. He recovers instantly, brings his head up, looks around, but then repeats the whole process again."

"What the heck?" said Phil, observing Red. "Never heard of that happening."

After three or four more times, Red drooped and toppled over, then woke up and rolled onto his chest. A few minutes later, the horse got up and grazed.

"The hell!" Phil said. "It's like he passes out. I'll ask Angus." He picked up the phone and called Angus Sheehan.

"HELLO . . . PHIL . . . ST . . . CLAIR," said Angus, his phone greeting always sounding like the baritone voice on Mr. Ed. "What can I do for you?"

Phil described what he'd seen, hoping for an answer. In our eyes, the Sheehans had decades of ranching knowledge compared to our, well, year.

"Uh huh. Yup. Hummmm."

"So," Phil asked him, after five minutes detailing everything about the Red's incident as best he could. "Is it something familiar to you?"

"Well," said Angus. "Sounds like he has narcolepsy."

"Phil, I just asked Rafe," said Lana Anderson, now on the party line. "He agrees."

"Huh? Oh," said Phil, slightly startled. "Thank you, Lana."

"Phil," chimed in Julia Gallagher. "It is probably narcolepsy."

"Okay," Phil said. "Thank you all for giving me advice on this." Phil wasn't positive they'd heard him because the chatter went on between the neighbors about their different horse problems, and they forgot about Phil.

Over the next few days, Red appeared to be normal, so Phil rode him to move some cattle. Everything was copasetic, unless Phil stopped the horse for five minutes, and then Red would pass out again and fall down. Phil narrowly missed getting crushed as the horse dropped from underneath him.

But, Phil did ride him for a few more years, always mindful of the possibility of another occurrence, but the attacks gradually went away.

Strangely, a similar event happened at the start of a lovely spring season when another of Pop's geldings started swaying and shaking his head. He would lurch and stagger into the fence or the willow trees. We didn't want to lose him so, we called Angus Sheehan.

"Well," he said, after his bellowing greeting. "I'm sorry to hear that Phil . . . St. . . . Clair. Sounds like brain fever; comes from mosquitoes. You can try to give him antibiotics, but it never works, really. Almost always fatal. Sorry."

Phil still gave it a try because we had some on hand and dosed him according to the instructions on the bottle. We stayed by his side, but lost him anyway. It was a devastating blow. With the loss of a horse, our incompetence level rose and showed its evil head. Having to deal with sickness and death up close was the worst part of working with horses or any other animal. The principal reason, I think, is they are so helpless and look toward their human companions for help.

The Sheehan family also had a quirky horse situation. When there was snow on the ground, they and the Hoffsteds rounded up some of their own mares that had been stolen by wild stallions. The work required superb riding skill, daring, and tenacity. John Sheehan rode a horse named Captain.

"Sometimes on a full-out run," said John, chuckling, "if Captain got hot and spied a snow bank, he'd slide to a stop and throw himself on it. After the second or third time, I knew it was coming, so I'd quickly step out of the stirrup before getting trapped."

In spite of Captain's peculiarity, John always rode him because he was so reliable the rest of the time. John's easy going personality always allowed him to maintain a good sense of humor about the odd trait. He rode Captain for many years, and the horse had a rich, full life.

***

Once in awhile, you encounter an ill-mannered horse. An example of this was another horse of Pop's, Madge, a feisty mare that had never been broken to ride.

"We can take the horses up Rosebud," I told my sister Paige, "and if we get into trouble, the dirt road will be better to land on than the highway."

Paige had just brought an old gelding, Mick, to the ranch and wanted to try him out on a longer outing. Of course, neither one of us was an experienced rider. Our combined confidence could fit on the head of a pin. At every weird move our horses made, we both screamed. Lucky for us, our horses were so elderly it didn't faze them.

"The only horses up here are Madge, Dave, and Dan," I said. "They shouldn't bother us."

I was on Joe, a sweet-tempered, old gelding Dad had bought years ago. Our two Australian Shepherds, Fat and Kallie, trotted happily beside us. As we reached the first meadow, the three horses whinnied and trotted in our direction. Our geldings ignored them, but the trio reached us and began biting and turning to kick our horses with their back legs. Paige and I tried to move our horses away from the commotion, but the trio kept attacking. We slid off our horses to avoid getting kicked or accidentally bucked off. Paige and I yelled and waved our arms. Finally, the horses ran off to the far end of the meadow.

"Should we go back?" I asked her, taking in huge gulps of air. "I'm not sure they won't follow us and try it again."

"Why did they attack us?" asked Paige, as if I knew the answer. Heck, she was older than I, and she was the one who traveled the rodeo circuit with our brother when she was a teen. But I'll take any part of appearing knowledgeable, especially when it's my sister. She'd always been *my* hero. Weird, but I experienced an unfamiliar feeling: Bravery. New for me.

"Not sure. Maybe because she's a mare," I said, remembering something like mares can sometimes cause trouble. I'd managed to retain that in my brain. Along with other useful things like, *stay off the moors. Stick to the road. Beware the moon.* But that really only applied to werewolves.

108

"Maybe you should lead the horses back," I said, "and I'll bring up the rear with the dogs, in case they come at us again."

Paige turned and started back but hadn't gone twenty yards before the other horses charged us. A sudden thought jammed into my head. I bent down to the dogs.

"Go get 'em!" My wonderful dogs, they'd never chased horses before, shot out, running full out, hugging the ground as they ran, straight at those horses—scaring them away and actually herding them up the draw.

My mouth drew flies as it hung open in amazement. My magnificent dogs came back, tongues lolling, but happy to be of service. You can bet they got some prime goodies when we got home.

***

Madge was always a little crazy. One night, while galloping madly around the pasture behind our Rosebud house, she collided with a large willow clump and jammed a broken limb into her chest. It never totally healed even after the vet treated it twice. This mare was not friendly, no matter how much we doted on her.

Madge redeemed herself when Pop decided to have her bred, and she produced a sweet, good-natured filly. Her name was Nugget. Phil wanted to work the yearling filly from the beginning to learn how to train this horse. While she was still a young horse, Phil gently encouraged her to come up the stairs on our deck, walk over piles of juniper logs, load in the trailer, have a saddle put on her back, pick up her feet, and all the usual things that scare horses. Nugget took to it all easily; she proved to be a quick learner. When she grew to a certain stage, Phil knew he needed a knowledgeable trainer to take her further. He searched for a person in the area, finally settling on the wife of a friend.

"I want the horse trained to ride," Phil, explained to Willow Spears. "Nothing harsh, but still guided."

Willow, a tall beautiful woman, nodded. "Phil," she said. "That's exactly how I feel about dealing with a new, young horse. Don't worry."

We both felt great when we drove home, except I decided to go with Phil whenever he had to return. Willow was just too pretty, and I had to watch over my man. I know, I'm ridiculous. I don't care.

A series of negative events occurred that turned Nugget into an angry horse. She got a bad barbed-wire fence wound that Willow tended everyday. When Nugget was healing nicely, Willow left her husband, so we had to move Nugget. We sent her to a series of folks who worked horses: but Nugget no longer trusted people, and she couldn't be trusted to ride because she acted up easily. We learned later that she had been used as a rodeo bucking horse. Phil vowed to never let a horse go through that again.

One of our best geldings came to us from a famous, local buckaroo couple. In their youth, Stark and Lula Swenson wrangled and trained young horses from horse-babyhood to work cattle on a ranch. Dad bought a gelding, Sandy, from them. Sandy was exceptional. The gelding became Phil's horse. They worked as a team for fifteen years. When Sandy passed on, Phil cried like a baby.

These animals and countless others, though they're gone now, stay forever in our hearts. Remembering them brings quick, hot tears to our eyes. All of them taught us how to be humane.

ഇഇഇ

Running with Animals

The grass behind the little house was three inches tall and deep green. Spring was here. No patches of snow, just Kentucky bluegrass sprouts. For the first time in my life, the thought crossed my mind that exercise might be necessary. After all, in July another year would be gone, and the big twenty-eighth birthday stared me in the face. *Old.* The body needed workouts to keep the machinery going smoothly. Phil needed it, too, and he would be excited about the decision to join me on the road every day.

"Huh?" Phil scowled at me. "I'm a young pup. I've worn the same size pants since high school, and that was only a couple of years ago." The pottery cookie jar was open, and Phil dug out a few pralines while he talked.

"You're going to be thirty in a few days," I told him, as I put the lid back on the jar. "So far, our bellies haven't shown up, but I expect them any day. If we start now, we might keep them from growing." Couldn't help it, but the picture in my head was of the movie, *Alien*, with something foreign growing inside my stomach, stretching and pushing, eventually to erupt into baby aliens.

"What kind of exercise?"

"Jogging. On the road."

"You mean where the neighbors drive by?" Phil said. "In front of *ranchers*?"

"Yep," I said. "What do we care what they think. We'll be getting healthy. Please, please, please? I'll jog down that lonesome highway alone if I have to, even though Ted Bundy is supposed to be roaming the highways looking for young women like me: defenseless women, unaccompanied, and wearing alluring running shorts and skimpy tops. But don't worry. I'll be okay by myself. All alone. In the dark—"

"In the dark?" Phil interrupted. "You know you're not going out in the dark."

"Yeah, okay. I got carried away."

Phil studied me, trying to gauge if he could win the debate. "Let's do it for a while," he said. "But if it cuts into too much of my work time, we'll have to stop."

111

I handed the cookie jar back to Phil. He could eat them all if he wanted to because he would exercise them off.

The next morning, I rolled out of bed eager to start. Homemade pancakes, eggs, maple syrup, and slab bacon made up our breakfast. Phil came out of the bathroom still yawning.

"Jeez, this looks great!" he said looking down at the feast. "Guess I made the right decision, huh?" His usual oatmeal paled in comparison. He was a happy guy.

As we slurped our last drops of coffee, I jumped up. "Ready?"

Belle and Whitewater knew something was up and milled around the kitchen by our feet. The huskies were always primed for action. Earlier I'd put on different clothes, not jeans and a shirt, and the dogs had their first clue that something was different. My pants were stretchy and loose, the top a sweatshirt, and my socks thick. Tennis shoes, *Keds®*, were the only running shoes I owned.

"I'll wait for you outside, okay?" The dogs and I played stick while waiting for Phil. By the time he wandered out, the dog stick was a slobbery mass of chewed wood. Phil had on his everyday clothes—jeans, shirt, and boots. Neither one of us had a clue about running shoes or clothes.

"Shall we take the dogs?" I asked. "Can we keep them off the road if a car comes?"

"Yeah," said Phil. "We'll just call them to us and hold on to their collars."

Stretching or warming up wasn't part of our exercise—we just threw ourselves into it.

"Let's go!" I shouted, "Come on girls! Phil, how about a race? Whoever gets to the schoolhouse first makes dinner?"

"Nah," said Phil, "Not interested. Let's just try to get through this."

The dogs immediately started prancing around us. We headed west down the yellow line. After a brisk few hundred yards, we noticed extra movement on each side of us. Our two cats, Big Orange and Mouse, had joined us.

"Gosh," I panted, "I didn't know cats liked to jog." Phil shrugged his shoulders as best as he could while bouncing up and down. Behind the meadow fence line, the horse whinnied and galloped, following us along the highway.

"Jeez," I gasped. "We've probably already gone a mile." A quick peek backwards and I saw the house maybe six hundred yards away.

"Are we moving or standing still?"

112

The highway took us past a rock outcropping on our corner. Pebbles sprinkled down on to the highway. A bleating sound came from up on its ninety-degree cliff. Our goats gamboled on one-inch ledges and fissures, leaping around on the face of the cliff.

"Good golly!" I wheezed. "The goats are defying gravity." While mesmerized by the goats, I stumbled into Phil, who had stopped to stare at them.

"OOF!" he said, holding me up to prevent me from taking an asphalt header. "Do you think they'll follow us the whole way?"

"Have no idea. I'm still amazed at our cats."

As we pulled away from the cliff, the goats angled downward, clearing the barbed-wire fence and onto the road in front of us. Immediately they started dropping pellets, so we jumped and dodged around them, inadvertently getting a better workout than we'd intended. Sort of a Mohammed Ali-type training exercise. Once in a while, a cat slowed in front of us, causing us to hop over them. A pattern emerged, and we suspected they got in front of us to slow us down and maybe even give up and turn back toward home.

"C'mon guys," I said, gasping for air. "If you're with us, you gotta give it your all, like we are."

Phil slackened and stopped to examine something squashed on the road.

"Aha!" I said, seeing his ruse for what it was. "You want me to get interested so you and the animals can leave me in the dust. Because squished bugs on the road fascinate me, your ploy is to slow me down, right?"

"No, really, Kristy. I've never seen a beetle with such horrendous claws or pincers!"

I stopped dead. It was too much. Phil knows that a squished bug *with* claws and pincers is just too fascinating for me to ignore. Also, he had his sincere voice on, so I took a chance and walked back to him. All the animals followed, forming a weird circle on the highway.

"Look. See?"

I bent down to examine the treasure and found—nothing.

"HAH!" yelled Phil as he vaulted over me and ran for all he could down the road. The animals and I looked up. The goats decided they liked the new game and also used me as their Olympic hurdle, then followed Phil.

The remaining group and I took off after them, running like the wind. Well, took off isn't the right term. The cats sauntered because they were

113

cool. The dogs yipped and shot after Phil, leaving the cats and me in their dust.

My braids were askew and flapping crazily when I caught up. Phil never smoked, so his wind was high and available. Mine was, too, but the explosive sprint cost me. Even so, we both had a deranged look for the effort. Then we heard an engine. Phil sneaked a peek over his shoulder. Rafe Anderson and his hired hands were driving up behind us. The goats were frolicking madly, the horse was still running up and down the other side of the fence line, and Big Orange and Mouse were traveling merrily next to us.

"You two need a ride?" asked Rafe, shifting the chew in his mouth. "Plenty of room in the back of the pickup for two goats, two cats, two dogs, and you two. Not the horse, though."

"Thanks, no," Phil said. "We're taking the animals for a walk, but they wanted to run, heh, heh, heh."

"Yeah," I said. "We're just fine. Thanks, though." We threw our heads back, straightened our shoulders, and stepped out lively. As if we did this every day.

"Okay," said Rafe, "but we'd be happy to come back on down the road to see if you need a ride back home."

In unison, we said, "No."

I added, "No. Really. Don't let us keep you from your chores."

Phil edged up the speed, and I matched it. Pretty soon we began an all-out run (instead of our original lazy jog). The truck kept pace alongside us.

"Wal, have fun and don't do nuthin' we wouldn't do! Hahahaha!" They took off, and after five more minutes of running, we watched them disappear around the corner.

We collapsed. The animals, left behind when we took on a burst of speed to show our neighbors how healthy we are, finally caught up to us. As we lay on the ground, heaving and gulping for air, they sniffed us all over. Maybe wondering if we were in the middle of our death throes. I wondered, too.

"Boy!" I said. "We've probably gone at least two miles. Especially that last powerful thrust."

Phil looked around. We'd made it to the first telephone pole—only about an eighth of a mile from our house.

"Well," I said. "If we hadn't worried about the animals getting tired, it would have been a different story!"

None of the animals had a tongue lolling, a chest heaving, or were lying on the ground. Probably because we took it easy. For them.

∞∞∞

ROLLING STOCK

It's the way you ride the trail that counts...
~Roy Rogers

Even if you're on the right track you'll get run over
if you just sit there...
~Will Rogers

Crawlers and Pickups

Eisenhower was still president when Dad's ranch rigs rolled off the line. One was a nifty little 1952 army green International Harvester, four-wheel drive flatbed truck with homemade wooden side racks. It was a straight six-cylinder vehicle and newly refurbished by a car buff in town.

On a spring day, we drove it up Dry Soda to take salt to Dad's cows in the Malheur National Forest. The dirt road had an elephant-size mud puddle near an aspen stand. We bumped and jerked around it, traveling to an ancient jeep trail fashioned by hunters and ranchers.

The pickup side-hilled across a ridge saddle, lumbering slowly until we reached a rocky knob. The road took us to the downhill side that was tip-over-sideways-steep. Finally at the salt place, it leveled. The return trip was steep *and* uphill with the cavernous maw on *my* side now. At the halfway point, the truck screeched and clunked, lost its forward momentum and rolled backwards. Phil rammed both feet hard on the brake, but it kept rolling.

"God!" he said, panting. "Don't know if I can stop it."

Behind and down to the left, a lone fifteen-foot juniper grew on a small, slightly more level spot. Phil whipped the wheel and backed into the tree. The truck stopped. My appreciation for Phil sparked anew. Married folks everywhere should remember those precious appreciation-morsel moments during arguments. Hopefully, Phil also has had those moments about me, but it's doubtful since I'm more cranky.

"What stopped us?" I whispered, still covered in awe over Phil's feat and, well, his feet. "Are we off the hill?"

"You can look now, Kristy," said Phil. "We've stopped. I don't know what happened. Maybe the truck slipped out of gear."

My eyes automatically close whenever danger threatens. It's my chicken tendency. Eyes shut mean nothing bad can happen. In this case, I opened them only to see blue sky in front of us and the Grand Canyon miles below— perfect for ski-crazed Olympians, but not for me.

Phil shifted the truck into four-wheel drive low and backed it up the slope. The maneuvering was going well until we hit a steeper part and spun out. Phil, always hopeful, backed down the hill again, this time in rear-wheel drive, and the truck wouldn't move. Only the front-wheel drive worked.

"We're gonna die," I moaned. "We haven't made our wills. Do you have a pen? I could write it on our arms. Although, if our arms get chopped off when the truck rolls over and over and over—"

"I have a plan," said Phil. "We'll walk to the ranch and get the crawler to pull us up and out."

"I don't think we can get out of this deathtrap without shifting the rig and causing it to roll over and over and over—"

Phil hopped out like we were back on flat ground. Then he came around and pulled me out. As if on tenterhooks, I tiptoed away from the truck. Phil had already reached the top of the hill so I followed, not wanting to be alone with the now, evil conveyance.

Six miles later, after a bracing walk back to the ranch house, we retrieved the ranch D-6 Crawler, and lurched and clunked back to the broken rig. When Phil paused on the peak, I hopped off to walk before we came upon the steep descent.

"Will you drive this and steer while I pull you to the top of the hill?" Phil asked, "You know you'll have to drive it around the steep side hill, right? So go slow."

I nodded. I could be brave...sometimes. Usually when Phil's life was in jeopardy. It was a breeze. And neither one of us died that day. Later, Phil successfully fixed the broken truck.

When I look back, for two citified people, we got a lot of stuff done with the help of Dad's antediluvian ranch rigs and grit—that is, Phil's grit. I am, and shall always remain, a fraidy cat.

***

A ranch rig is vital when constructing a new fence—specifically, in getting to the fence location with all the equipment involved. The back of the rig has to hold rolls of wire, wire stretchers, staples, hammers, pliers, wooden stays, metal posts, a post pounder, chain saw, gas and oil for the saw, sharpener for the chain, extra chain, shovel, pick axe, large clippers, small clippers, coats, rain gear, baling twine, old hay, two or three dogs, water for dogs, ice chests for drinks, snacks, sandwiches, and ice. Also, if we had any visiting relatives or friends, a bigger ice chest with more stuff in it, extra dogs and additional dog water, cameras, books (for lunch time), interesting rocks and boulders, and old crushed beer cans. In other words, you have to take almost everything that you'd need to set up another home. Although you think you've packed everything in an orderly fashion, going up steep hills throws all of it into a soup against the tail gate. Steep hills are the norm in Izee, and aged ranch vehicles aren't always serviced every year, so the brakes aren't reliable. Phil never mentioned that part when we set out to do one of the creepiest fences in history. My history, anyway.

"You know that fence Jim's been helping me build between Soda and Poison?" Phil asked. "On that sheer hillside?"

"Y-yes," I gulped. The breakfast ham stuck in my throat. I slugged down some hot coffee, quickly. After a near fatal choking episode that ended with Phil pounding my back and getting ready to Heimlich me, I gurgled, "What about it?"

"Well, Jim's leaving for a while, right?" he said, wiping coffee off my cheek, "So I'll need your help."

He must really be desperate, I thought. "Okay, but you know that I'm as useful as a third breast on a baseball," I said. "What can *I* do?"

"First of all, that makes no sense, but it *is* thought provoking," he said. "And, second, you can carry stuff that wears me down."

Even though I flunked Fencing Skills 101, I was pretty good at hauling miscellaneous objects around for Phil. Plus, being outdoors and helping Phil always made my heart soar like an eagle. Both Bald and Golden. Really. But if I knew about the "hill," I would have passed. Oh, all right. I wouldn't have, but it brought out the *heebie jeebies* in me, whatever *they* are.

The Chevy truck rumbled up Old Car Draw (aptly named for all the junked old cars—and bearing an uncanny resemblance to the Appalachians and all that comes with that lore). Finally, we stopped at the base of Mount Kilimanjaro. A fit of sneezing, coughing, and intermediate gulping seized me. Once again, Phil thumped me on the back, still hoping he could give me the Heimlich. Probably because he'd never done it on anyone, and it's kind of cool.

"Hey! Ow!" I said. "Stop it! Stop it," I said. "Sheesh! You'll maim me, and I'll end up like Igor with a lump on my back."

"Sorry," he said. "Don't want my fencing pard to die before we start. Hang on."

Phil put it in four-wheel and started up the mountain. Our ranch dogs, Riz and Dollie, had already jumped out and were chasing squirrels. Objects in the back crashed together.

"What—? Phil, please let me walk."

"Too late, sweetie, we've already started, so I can't stop yet."

Before I could shut my eyes, the landscape looked like what the astronauts see on take-off: a vertical world. My legs almost touched my chest. My eyes slammed shut, and my hands closed over them. The engine

119

labored as it snailed up the slope. Halfway up, it stalled. Phil threw it in first and hit the hand brake with his foot. The rig slipped back slightly.

I jumped out. Phil looked at me with his hound dog eyes, so I jumped back in. If we were gonna die, we would do so together.

"Don't worry," he said, smiling. "I've got this. Happens all the time." He turned the key, and working the clutch, brake, and gas pedals, he got it going again. The truck slugged on up the slope. We parked at each work spot (still creepy after all these years) and in a week, finished the slope. The fence was straight and true.

On another occasion, we were cutting and splitting juniper for firewood to sell in John Day. It was winter, and the snow was twelve inches deep. Phil worked on the D-6, dragging juniper trees down close to where I sat in the pick-up directly below him. Phil turned the crawler across the hillside, and it started to slide down sideways because of the snow. He's patient and stubborn, so he maneuvered as best as he could with only one side of the brakes working.

At the end of the day, we attended a program at the Izee School. We sat next to Ernst Hoffsted, a neighbor from Izee. Phil casually told Ernst that we'd just finished dragging in a load of juniper with the old crawler. The man's face blanched.

"What did you say, Phil?" he said, his voice shaking. "You worked on a steep, snow-covered hill with that old crawler of yours, and Kristy was below you in the truck? Phil, if you get a crawler sideways on a snowy hill, it can take off like a sled, hit a stump, and flip over. Promise me, you kids won't do that again. You'll likely die if you do. All kinds of things could happen! Good God Almighty!"

ࠦࠦࠦ

Ranch Rigs

For a spring morning in Izee, it was unusually warm. It seemed all the birds in the world had come to perch in our willows to sing to us. During breakfast, I realized I'd used the last of the eggs and bread. We had to do a grocery run.

"Gotta go to town," I said to Phil. "We need food."

"I can't go, Kristy," Phil said. "Wade, Owen, Jeff, and I are moving cows. Wade and I volunteered to ride, so when we have to move our cows, others will help us. You know, the help-for-help thing?"

"Heck!" I said. "That means I go alone in that awful Wagoneer?"

"Sorry. We have to help them."

Later, I grumped around while putting on my town clothes. Actually town clothes were the same garments I wore on the ranch: jeans, shirt, and sandals. Oh, and underwear. Even as a hippie, I never went without the underthings— well, except a bra. I hate bras!

Anyhow, when I was finally on the road entering Bear Valley, I felt something run across my feet. I had on a pair of our handmade sandals, so I knew something *alive* was down there. At first, it felt like a breeze passing over my toes, but then it happened again. Little feet.

"EEEEEE!" I yelled, as I pulled off the road. Then I felt a tiny nibble. "Eeek! I squealed, jerking my feet around. "Eeeeek. Get away!" Strange, but instead of immediately searching for what I thought to be a critter, I actually screamed, "Eeeeek!" instead. No one really does that except in books, yet here I was doing it. Sudden activity below brought me out of my pondering. The little rascal did it again.

I jumped out and looked everywhere—under seats, window shades, and rugs. Nothing. Should I go back home or to town? What if it happened again and I wrecked the car? Did I have a fresh pair of undies on in case that last scenario happened? My family had a horror of getting into a wreck while wearing day-old panties for all the ambulance and medical personnel to see and judge.

The Wagoneer sat for long periods of time, so it probably had a nest of mice in it somewhere. Yuck. Still, I needed food, and I'd do almost anything to eat. I scooted back in and headed for town and doughnuts. Without incident, I'm happy to say.

121

The local grocery store, Chester's, was packed with cart-pushing shoppers. Unfamiliar faces strolled by. The loudspeaker squawked.

"Will the owner of the green Wagoneer please move their vehicle from the parking lot? It is leaking gas and endangering people around it."

That poor person, I thought. How awful to have someone's car troubles broadcasted so publicly. Wait a minute. That's me! Oh gosh! I strolled casually toward the door in Nancy Drew fashion, hopefully acting inconspicuous, until I got outside and assessed the situation.

"There she is!" yelled a stranger, pointing her unusually long finger at me. "She did it!"

Luckily nobody saw her encouraging my capture. A quick, furtive, this-isn't-mine look at the Wagoneer proved that, sure enough, gas was flowing out from under the rig.

Two store employees hovered over the jeep shaking their heads. An unruly crowd gathered, yelling questions to the men.

"We're all gonna die!" screamed one mother while clutching two toddlers to her breast. "It's gonna blow!" More voices joined in, and I might have heard someone shouting "Find a rope! We'll have ourselves a hangin'!" but maybe not. I was pretty frazzled, but I made a sudden bold— okay, more chicken-ish than bold—move and rushed past the grocery guys.

"It's mine! Oh, thank you for finding it for me. Somebody stole it! Thank God I have an extra pair of keys! Oh, and in the store I saw a grungy, dirt-caked, and smelling of gas, drug user. Maybe he stole it. Could you guys call the police and go find him? Meanwhile I'll head on home."

By that time I didn't care if the car blew up; I just wanted outta there. Me and my car mouse. Strange bedfellows and all that. I looked in the rear view mirror and, in my mind, the people had become a mob, holding pitchforks and axes and dancing around a bonfire.

On the next trip into town, mouse and I would be incognito and drive a different rig. Or a rig with a repaired gas tank.

***

As we slogged our way through a variety of old and beat up rigs, it's not surprising that mishaps occurred. Our first ride in Izee was our hippy Volkswagen bus. Its heater broke early on because the previous owner was a stoner/piano virtuoso/well-known Portland painter. He ignored the VW's problems and also the rules of the road because he was often high. You can't mosey down a seventy-mile-an-hour freeway at forty miles per

122

hour without consequences. So the bus had lots of nicks and dents as well as non-functioning equipment. One of those things was a broken heater.

On a trip back from Portland in the winter, we brought more stuff over to the ranch; Phil had rented a small U-Haul truck, while Wade and I drove the van. We had icicles coming out of our drippy noses it was so frigid. We wondered if we'd ever thaw out. The van had so many problems, and we were just too poor at the time to get them repaired, so we sold it.

On another journey into town, we bought a dirt-cheap, blue International Harvester Scout. It didn't have carpeted floors, which was good for living on a ranch. It was one of the first SUVs in Izee.

One late winter's eve, driving home on snowy roads, we arrived at the long downgrade of Izee Summit. The extreme curves would have made Mae West envious. We always slowed at the top because of the possibility of black ice on the highway. Deep canyons with the snowy tops of massive fir, pine, and tamarack on the right and towering forested banks on the left sheltered the highway, leaving frozen, slick roads. Phil usually drove until, eventually, I felt confident enough.

"Uh oh," Phil said, pumping the brake. "Hold on, Kristy. The brakes don't work."

"Wha—?" I squeaked out. I'd been napping. "Is this a dream? You're not Elvis."

The Scout was already rolling and gaining momentum, but Phil took it out of third and quickly shifted down to second gear. The car jerked back, slid a bit and slowed, but it still moved at thirty miles-per-hour. Sleep and Elvis vaporized, leaving a solid lump deep in my stomach. The road reflected bright in the headlights and glistened like a black river. It was ice.

Phil hugged the center line away from the steep cliff on the right as we took each curve, hoping for no oncoming traffic. After completing one curve, we'd breathe out, but going into the next one, we'd hold our breath again. The road gradually evened out and got less precipitous, but that still didn't keep the Scout wholly stable. It slipped and slid all the way down from the summit, but Phil managed to keep us steady and safe.

"Phew!" he said, breaking the granite wall of tension that had settled inside the Scout. "Just wasn't sure we'd make it. Don't have that much experience driving on ice anyway, and then adding to the equation, coasting down a steep cliff in a car with no brakes."

"You did great," I said. "What a nerve-racking situation. It's weird, but I kept thinking about that dream I had when I was seventeen. You know, the one where I flew like a bird over the ground, and ahead of me the curvy road straightened when I got near, and the high bumps smoothed out. Then when we became Christians, I found it in the Bible in Isaiah and Luke. It said, 'Every valley shall be filled in, every mountain and hill made low. The crooked roads shall become straight, the rough ways smooth.' Well, maybe that's what sort of happened. Who knows?"

***

While we had the Wagoneer, its presence contributed to a number of weird adventures. One involved goats.

Our animal guru, Nita, always worked on us to get goats and raise them for slaughter. Goats had to be either tied to a spot to graze or let out to roam free. They ate weeds like nettles, and dandelions which threatened to engulf us. We allowed the goats to munch around the driveway because the weeds also hid the Wagoneer.

In summer, we left the Wagoneer's doors open to air it out. One day I looked out and saw movement in the front seat. I ran out to see. The goats had climbed in and enjoyed the dashboard, steering wheel, and the upholstery. In between car noshing, they pooped and piddled everywhere. As it happens, the goats and the Wagoneer went the way of vampires in sunlight. They were gone in short order—both too smelly and costly to keep.

ᏬᏬᏬ

GOD STUFF

If there is no God, who pops up the next Kleenex?
~Art Hoppe

God enters by a private door into each individual...
~Emerson

Hippies Find Jesus in Izee

"Phil, there's a gathering of Buddhists because the Roshi's coming to town," said Garth, one of our fellow Red Balloon Gallery dwellers—all artists/beatniks of one kind or another. "You and Kristy want to come? We have to leave at two a.m."

"Yeah!" Phil said. "Groovy. What's a Roshi?"

"He's a famous Zen Master from Japan. This same Roshi was with the Beatles," said Garth. "He'll enlighten us."

Later, in the privacy of our home, Phil sprung it on me.

"Nope," I told him. "At two a.m., I'll be under warm covers. Besides, that lecture at Reed College by that Yogi guy in the white turban had us looking at our poop to see if it floated. Made going to the bathroom a complicated process. No. Don't think so."

"Okay, I'll go by myself. Garth said that lots of beautiful women will be there."

"What time is Garth picking us up?"

These are the hippie days, before our move to Izee. Christianity, Hinduism, Buddhism, Taoism, Dadaism, Paganism, and other *isms*— none of them interested me. Religion offered nothing but airy beliefs that took advantage of needy people by perpetuating falsehoods while robbing their pocket books. Not that I harbored any strong opinions about the subject or anything. But for some reason unknown to me, Phil was interested in this stuff.

Crotchetiness settled on me. So, naturally I took it out on Phil. "Why can't they hold this event during normal hours? Is it a secret gathering? Do the participants wear devil masks and hooded robes? Is there dancing around granite obelisks? Are these people on posters at the post office? Maybe we ought not to associate with subversives or cultish folk."

Phil tied the leash of our pet raccoon, Bubalina, to the wooden porch railing behind the old Victorian house in northwest Portland. "Kristy, where's your spirit of adventure?" he said, a touch of disappointment tinged his voice. "It doesn't hurt to be enlightened. Are you wearing make-up?"

126

"No, course not." I said, bald-faced fibbing. Hippie women don't wear makeup. Truth was I tarted up a bit because of all the gorgeous women who were supposed to be there. I had to hold my own.

"Will Bubalina be safe here?" I asked, changing the subject.

Like lemmings, we plodded along with the other people entering the basement of the ancient, three-story house. Phil spied Manfred, a gallery owner we knew. Inside the large room, we crouched on thin mats laid in rows. Phil's mat sat acres away. I was just about to sneak over near Phil when a bell rang and everyone bowed forward, heads touching mats. I peeked and noticed a robed man moving up and down the aisles carrying a long, thin stick. What was that for? The bell rang twice, and everyone rose and danced between the mats. I had no choice but to join them. After all, dancing was my thing. It was risky because I knew I'd forget which mat was mine.

Meanwhile, although this worship went on for five lifetimes, I got my moves down—a bit of the Fly, the Funky Chicken, maybe some Locomotion thrown in. At the same time, I searched for Phil to give him a *get-me-outta-here* look, but in the dance-worshiping frenzy, I never saw him.

Again, the bell rang, this time three rings. Everyone flopped down. One mat was empty, so I assumed it was mine.

After the next bell, as we put our heads to the mat, I heard a THWACK!

"Aaaaaaaahooouch!!" My head shot up. The robed one had struck the backside of an innocent worshiper-person two rows over!

"Let me explain," said the Nazi disguised as a monk. "This is your helper, your physical spiritual guide." He pointed to the stick. "Should you fall asleep, it will wake you."

At that instant I knew—if he smacked me or Phil with that stick, he would find it put some place—into a main orifice—so fast he would beg to join his enlightened Buddhist buddies in Nirvana. I never took my eyes off him until lunch.

After the stick incident, another monk said we would singly visit the Roshi, or master, in a separate room. He had a special mantra for each person. Finally, it was my turn. A plump and bald Asian man resembling Buddha smiled from his cushiony perch and said, "When a horse walks a lonely road, where does it go?"

C'mon! That was it? What bull crappy. Their sound bites didn't even make sense.

127

Anyhow, released from detention at lunch, I elbowed my way to Phil and between clenched teeth told him Bubalina and I were going home, dammit. Phil looked dazed. Had they already gotten to him?

"Phil," I said, "Look into my eyes." He did. No wiggling pools of dark brown looked back at me, which, if they had, meant they'd messed with him according to all alien-hunters' guidebooks. Just in case, I slipped him some pertinent questions, conversationally.

"Well now, doesn't baldness look good on the Roshi—*When's my birthday?*" I whispered giving him a steely, penetrating look saved for just this type of situation.

"It's in June sometime."

"Where do you think we should eat—*How old are you?*"

"Um, let's see, you're twenty. . .uh . . .one, right? So I must be twenty-five."

Wrong answers, all. He never remembers those things. He got a big hug and wet kiss. It was definitely Phil.

Now that I no longer had to worry about Phil's mental state, I insisted we make like a banana and peel out of there. Edging to freedom along the rather hidden sidewalk next to the house, we walked by the kitchens and saw Manfred again.

"Isn't this the greatest?" he said. He was at the stove stirring an enormous pot of rice. "Lunch is coming up. As a token of reverence, we only eat plain rice during these meetings."

Phil turned as white as the rice in the pot. Even more than our normal hippie pallor. Rice was as popular to him as steamed cardboard. He pulled me out of earshot. "We're leaving." Oh, thank Buddha!

With great stealth, mentally thanking the specific rules from all the horror films we'd seen, we tiptoed past windows and entered an attached garden shed. It presented an alternative escape possibility. As we entered a side door, we navigated over rakes and hand mowers through to another exit. Freedom! Bubalina chirruped a surprised greeting, while Garth's booming laugh preceded his entrance through the front door on the porch above us. The Roshi followed behind him.

He pointed at Bubalina. "Badger?"

Garth chuckled, explaining our unusual pet. The group gaped at us. It looked as if we'd been made and that they were on to us, so Phil and I began yammering out excuses.

"Darn it, we need to be home when the septic-tank guy comes . . ."

"Yep, gotta go. We're serving dinner to the homeless at the nearby shelter on Burnside..." I felt guilty (for only a nanosecond) telling the small group this fib, but desperation took over. Phil's made-up excuse trumped mine.

Then we noticed they were leaving, too. Wasn't there still a half day left of deprivation, torture, and murky utterances? Along with plain rice?

Garth took us aside after the Roshi entered a silver-colored Mercedes Benz. "He wants to go to McDonald's for lunch," Garth said, a sheepish look on his face. "He hates rice."

Aha! So there it was: Religion in a nutshell. Like those television evangelists in their 10,000 square foot houses and white Cadillacs or, in the Roshi's case, a Mercedes. Why did gullible people follow them? Why did anyone need to know or even wonder about the *deep meaning of life* anyhow? It was not for me. Getting away from stifling religions and relocating to Izee sounded good. Ranchers seemed centered and basic. No pretend religion, just dirt and animals.

Then a couple of things happened before the migration to Izee. First, we saw two movies. The *Exorcist*, which presented a desolate, omnipotent evil, but which also sparked a burning need to be on the side of the good guys. And *Fiddler on the Roof*, that portrayed a reverence for Jewish people and their unwavering family-oriented, God-centered lives.

The second occurrence was a book we read. Books were gold in Izee because there were no television signals or boring radio stations. We devoured all types of books but preferred the dark novels by H.P. Lovecraft, Algernon Blackwood, and Stephen King. In fact, we were in the middle of the last Lovecraft novel when we decided he was too creepy and took it back to the library, even telling the librarian the book was truly evil. That was when my Mom suggested we read *The Late, Great Planet Earth* by Hal Lindsey. She didn't tell us it was a book about Christian prophecies.

***

A couple of months after moving to Izee, we became born-again Christians just from reading that book. No church, no preacher no fanfare, just a book. It caused a complete turnaround in our lives. Friends and family saw the change. I never, ever thought that would happen to me, someone who had *disdain* for everything religious. The ranch hippies were now holy rollers.

෭෭෭෭

Rancher's Bible Study

Word spread through the valley that the hippies had found Jesus, so we got invited to the Bible study held at the ranch next to ours. We were excited, but my nephew Wade cared less. He decided we'd changed into brainless followers like the characters in the movie, *Astro Zombies*. Sprawled on our couch, he watched us with squinty Clint Eastwood-like eyes.

"You want to go, Wade?" Phil said. "Folks would be blessed to see you."

"Your mother."

"Well, then, praise God." As a new Christian, Phil was getting the Jesus jargon down. We were determined to walk the talk.

"I think I'll just shine this one on."

"Okay. We'll pray for you."

"Up yours, homeboy."

"Oh, yeah? Well, God is good."

Wade snorted his reply. The usual goofiness we shared with Wade seemed frivolous in the sight of the Lord, so we tempered it just in case. The rules were still murky.

Then off we went, disappointed that our recent piousness hadn't converted Wade. It was amazing, I mean, he'd seen *The Exorcist* too. He'd gotten a glimpse of the dark side. Maybe he didn't understand that we had to be on the *good* side, not on the side of the devil.

However, the optimism of a new believer is infinite. We figured he'd get nailed sometime. Maybe if God sent one of those honking big angels like Michael or Gabriel knocking on our door while we were at the Bible study, Wade might change his mind—although that gang-kid background of his might lead him to tell God's messenger to 'stick it, homies'.

Our zeal overshadowed the fact that God does what He pleases in His own time, and we should back off. Wade was worth the wait. We reluctantly put Wade into God's hands and left for the study.

A few minutes later, we entered the Johnsons' mud room. From within their house, Cam and June Johnson called out a merry hello. Like everyone else, we removed a large percentage of our winter clothes. The area already held a lopsided mountain of old Stetsons splattered with dried afterbirth, cow poop, and mud. A couple of Sorel packs with the felt linings hung out for drying, and an enormous quantity of cowboy boots, smashed down from decades of feet slamming into stirrups and slogging up fence lines, lined the pine wall. Beside them lay black rubber, pointy-toed overshoes that ranchers wore over their cowboy boots. Carhart jackets were in even larger heaps. Their ripped pockets exposed tattered threads that snagged pocketknives, pickup keys, and two or three broken ChapStick tubes with fur, hay, and dirt stuck to them. As we shed our winter gear, snatches of rancher conversations drifted in from the living room.

"Got 'er in the chute and cut the son-of-a-gun off. Blood gushed out. Slapped a chunk 'o chew on it...was all I had. She'll live or die."

"Crappy weather, huh? Fed up Lonesome, today. Snow's so deep, I lost Shep when he jumped off the hay wagon. He caught up with us though."

"These cookies are so dang good! Lord almighty! I wish Georgia made these. She says I'm too fat and never intended on being married to two 'o me."

Cam decided it was time to open the study. He snatched his acoustic guitar. His son, Lance, brought up a fiddle, and moved into the fast melody. My four-chord plucking on the banjo caught the beat. Phil and I were singing fools even though we'd switched from tunes like Linda Ronstadt's bluesy "You're No Good," or the Eagles sad ballad "Lyin' Eyes," to the virtuous "I'm My Beloved and He is Mine."

Soon our new preacher arrived. Reverend Jarod Locust and his wife Mabel drove down from Hines, to lead the study. Reverend Locust, a delicate hairless man, wore a prim black cowboy hat, large black and white cowboy boots, and a robin's-egg blue polyester suit, cut cowboy style. Mabel, a woman as robust as her husband was slight, sported a sunflower-yellow floral dress with a white crocheted collar, sleeves and hem. She also wore open-toed yellow pumps in spite of the four inches of fresh snow outside.

June offered them the cushiony loveseat, but Reverend Locust veered off and settled on a tall wooden chair, plunking down an open bible on his lap. Mabel swooped onto the couch, whipped out her long knitting needles, a heap of something purple, chartreuse, and mud brown with gold flecks, and began click clacking with gusto. An instant image formed in my brain — of Madam La Farge from *The Tale of Two Cities,* knitting, while yelling "Guillotine! Guillotine!" The exertion gave her a sheen a

131

Victoria's Secret model would envy. As she worked, her mouth matched her activity: knit—puckered lips, purl—then relax. The preacher beamed down at her with love and then bowed his head in prayer, "Lord, please bless Your word. Amen."

He plunged into a twenty-minute, eye-drooping monotone. A couple of older ranchers, Guy Wainright and Ray Cornwell, snored in the back of the room. Guy yelled out in his sleep, "Git yur goldarn foot outta thet trough yew ugly flat-nosed beggar!" awaking two babies and the Johnsons' fifteen-year-old Persian cat, who was a blur of orange as it streaked out of the room.

The minister's hand snaked up Medusa-like to his ear. The index finger drilled deep within, and he droned on as if his hand wasn't his.

June touched Cam's arm.

"Let's all sing," Cam said. "C'mon now, don't be shy!" He whipped his guitar up and strummed out a rollicking "Bright Morning Stars are Shining," joined a second later by Lance, who tucked his violin under his chin, swooping the bow up and down over the strings and chasing the melody. Over a dozen voices, some better than others, lent their support, creating the best and truest choir.

After the song, Reverend Locust continued, "If your eye causes you to stumble, pluck it out and throw it from you." His hand lowered and flicked something underneath the chair. Twenty pairs of eyes involuntarily followed its path. A heartbeat or two passed when the ill-behaved hand began to mine the cavern of the other ear.

"What in the Sam Hill is he doin'?" mumbled Chuck Hoffsted. "If he goes any deeper, he'll reach China." Sitting against a back wall, he was out of earshot of the preacher. One of the little kids, perched on his parent's lap, started a finger towards his nose but his quick-thinking mom grabbed his little arm, gently cradling it back into his lap.

"But Mom," the tyke said, pointing at the preacher, "he—"

"God wants us to dig deeply in His word for He has treasures for us to mine," Reverend Jarod said. "In 2 Timothy 1:6, God says, 'For this reason I remind you to kindle afresh the gift of God which is in you through the laying on of my hands." Once again, *his* hand sought out the space under his chair, and he let fly. Mabel never looked up as wives will often do, performing covert signals about their mate's indiscretion, but she'd added two inches onto her knitting project.

My humor, inappropriate at the best of times, bubbled dangerously close to eruption. I felt Phil's shoulder's shaking while he bent over to retie his already-tied shoe. I peeked around my Bible and saw the rest of the group dealing with their own reactions. With effort, the younger ones looked at the walls, the floor, and the windows where snow was falling outside. Their parents' faces were beet red, each laying a warning hand on their children's shoulders. Ranchers dealt with animal detritus every day, but aside from an occasional fingernail scouring with their knives, they were always mannerly.

Cam chose the only way out: another song. Unfortunately, in his haste, Cam picked "Put Your Hand in the Hand of the Man from Galilee."

Soon after, we all said our goodbyes and thanked Reverend Jarod and his wife. In our new pious persona and with uncharacteristic insight, Phil and I decided it wasn't our call to judge the minister and his wife. Maybe the two were so comfortable in the company of our friendly Bible study they thought they were home.

Later in our kitchen, we told Wade about Reverend Jarod and Mabel. Swiping at his eyes after a hard bout of laughing, relief poured over his face. We were back and our mutual zany view of life, even as Christians, reassured him.

"Jeez, it's nice to know you guys can still laugh. I was worrying those days were over because you were getting so damned religious."

Recovering from his own guilt-ridden chuckle jag, Phil said, "Well, evidently God has a sense of humor to enlist Reverend Jarod and Mabel in sharing the gospel along with . . . er . . . other, more earthy things."

ଚ୍ଚଚ

About the Author

Although a fourth-generation Californian on her mother's side, Kristy came to Oregon when she was fourteen. At eighteen, she married Phil St. Clair, the boy she believed would put up with her and her odd family, and in the 1960s they began careers in Portland as hippie leather craftsmen and sandal makers in a craft gallery. Surrounded by older artists from the Beat Generation, the couple's apprenticeship was beyond price, with painters, potters, sculptors, and writers serving as their mentors. They sold their work at juried art-and-craft shows and participated in group shows as well as two-man and one-man gallery shows.

For the last three decades, instead of sipping Pinot Noir at gallery openings, they got to hunker sweat-soaked alongside streams after cattle drives, look down from a ridge on horseback and watch a bull elk fuss at his harem, or get spattered with afterbirth while hauling a sluggish calf out from its mother's back end. Along the way, Kristy acquired a college degree at Eastern Oregon University while at the same time driving Phil crazy helping him on the ranch. At some point, she realized writing was the best way to let readers know about Izee as well as the people who have influenced her life.

Kristy's first memoir, *Accidental Cowgirl, a City Slicker's Life on an Eastern Oregon Ranch*, was published in 2007 by Bear Creek Press of Wallowa, Oregon, with a second printing in 2009. Her articles have appeared in *Cowboy Magazine* ("Cowboying in Eastern Oregon," Summer 2003); *Range Magazine* ("Buckaroo Wisdom," Spring 2004 and "The Indomitable Spirit of Kate Jordan," Fall 2004); *American Western E-zine* ("Corral Savvy," 2003); *Hallowzine* ("Hunting Fate," 2002); and the *Blue Mountain Eagle* ("The Hunting," 2001).

Made in the USA
Charleston, SC
10 November 2016